GIFT *of* TIME

GIFT *of* TIME
— A MAY-DECEMBER ROMANCE —

Peter E. S. Nichols

GIFT *of* TIME
A May-December Romance
Copyright © 2016 Peter E.S. Nichols

All rights reserved. No part of this book may be used or reproduced in any form, electronic or mechanical, including photocopying, recording, or scanning into any information storage and retrieval system, without written permission from the author except in the case of brief quotation embodied in critical articles and reviews.

Cover Photograph: Charlotte, circa 1932
Book Designed by The Troy Book Makers
Printed in the United States of America

The Troy Book Makers • Troy, New York • thetroybookmakers.com

To order additional copies of this title, contact your favorite local bookstore or visit www.tbmbooks.com

ISBN: 978-1-61468-364-3

For Charlotte

Acknowledgements

I am grateful, first, for the unwavering help of my Kent writers' group: Harmon Smith, Tora Givotovsky, Earl Brecher, and Rik Barberi. Early on, Marian Thurm encouraged my initial impulse, and Karen Novak believed ardently in my book. At the Bennington Writing Seminars, Askold Melnyczuk, Jill McCorkle, and Lynne Sharon Schwartz helped me develop the manuscript. And later, Patricia Horan helped me bring my book to fruition.

For a book like this, written largely in secret, I must thank good friends who, by accepting Charlotte and me as a couple, indirectly gave me the courage to write.

Among them are Frank Tocco, Keith and Wendy Krizan, Joel Foster, Tonia Shoumatoff, Mary Busch, Ivy Farinella, and Lew Koch. And my loving family, sisters Suzanne Nichols and Elspeth Whitney, and brother-in-law Charles Whitney.

For her love, patience, and encouragement, most of all I thank Betty.

"[S]he became a friend for life, nearest to my heart, and the person I treasured and understood more than anyone else. It was her unselfish love of the world that enriched me and nourished me with the strength I would need for the hard life that lay ahead."

Maxim Gorky, *My Childhood*

Contents

Part 1

Weird Old Relic — 1
A Kiss That Changed Everything — 9
Country Charlotte — 21
Portrait of the Analyst — 27
Making a Living — 33
The Best Eggs — 39
Island Insight — I Love Her — 45
Eros and Ashes — 59
My Proposal — 65
Venice Mysteries — 71
Groom 39, Bride 86 — 77
A Cooking Lesson — 81
The Money Angle — 83
A Dinner and a Vow — 87
The Wedding Dream — 93

Part 2

Charlotte's Family — 101
A Break That Binds — 109
You're Living Too Old — 115
Rewards of Success — 123
My Father's Eyes — 127
Reconciliation — 131

Part 3

Idyll of Kent — 139
Gone Fishing — 149
Poems and Paintings — 153
My Affair — 157

Part 4

A Fall at the Opera — 165
Goodbye to the Doctor — 169
Time's Losses — 173
Temptation — 183
Saving Graces — 189
Sunset of Butterflies — 195

Afterword — 201
Sketches of Charlotte — 203

Introduction

Charlotte's eyes were bright as a fox's, radiating intelligence. Her straight white hair was stylishly cut in a gentle curve. Though angled with age, her hand held a martini firmly. She had hips as slim as a girl's, and her legs were firm all the way down to solid feet with perfect arches, like a dancer's. Charlotte was beautiful well into her nineties. And she was mine.

I'd like to think that our love story—starting when I was in my thirties and she in her eighties—is unique, but I haven't taken a poll. What I do know is that our hands fit perfectly together as we lay in bed. That we trusted each other.

Now I can tell about the intimacy that we kept a secret from virtually everyone, even as Charlotte neared the age of one hundred.

In a sense I stole a half-century of time, from her birth in 1902 to mine in 1949, because through her eyes I learned about the *Titanic* and flappers, the Depression and the two world wars that separated us. She gave me an extra past, and I gave her a more youthful future.

Charlotte is the hero of this story, a woman who bravely restarted and re-created her life—with me. But she never changed her essential self, because she always knew exactly who she was. As well as her love, her crystal clarity was her great gift to me.

I was a young man in need of direction and purpose, ambitious in some ways, timid in others. Charlotte had danced with F. Scott Fitzgerald and walked in Spain with Ernest Hemingway, but she was most happy with me. After her marriages, to a writer and then an artist, *I won her* in the end. If I attain nothing else in my life, I have loved an extraordinary woman.

PART 1

1

Weird Old Relic

On a summer day in 1981, my father opened a show of his paintings in the back of the House of Books, in the small rural town of Kent, Connecticut. I considered my father a professional failure, because after a lifetime of painting, this was his only one-man show. But of course I came to the opening. The little bookstore was crowded with people.

Visual art was a family affair, since my mother and I were also artists. I had grown up watching my parents paint in their studios whenever they wanted, never having to leave the house to do a day's work for money. If only modestly, they were independently wealthy.

Not that I thought about it all the time, but here was my problem: I grew up privileged, but the privilege hadn't gone far enough. I envied my parents. I wouldn't get trust fund checks like my father did. I loved art, too, but I taught freshman composition in Manhattan. I was thirty-two years old but had not made my mark in any real way.

I stood alone with a plastic cup of Merlot in my hand, out on the sidewalk in front of the House of Books. For a few minutes, I was avoiding people. I wasn't exactly socially paranoid, but I often felt inhibited in social settings, and so I wanted a time-out. The sidewalk offered a respite.

As I drank my wine, a black limousine pulled up, and a slender, white-haired old woman stepped out. She wore a straight-brimmed straw hat with a red ribbon around its crown, the word VENEZIA emblazoned on the ribbon. In a leopard skin coat, she seemed to be proving that she dressed as she pleased.

Looking agitated, nervous, she pulled a pack of cigarettes out of her little black purse, lit up, and puffed aggressively before she noticed me.

"You're Peter."

Did I know the old lady?

She stepped toward me.

"I'm your father's cousin Charlotte," she informed me. "When you were a child, I saw you running around and around on the old floors in your house near here."

Yes, she'd visited when my parents bought the 1791 saltbox five miles up a hill in Kent. We'd once had dinner at her apartment in Manhattan, and a long time ago, I'd attended a big art show of her husband's in the city.

"Do you know why I'm late getting here from the city?" she said, stepping closer. "My driver got us lost. Now he's inside at your father's show drinking up all the wine!"

There was something conspiratorial in the way she spoke. Why was this weird old lady confiding in me?

"I had to come," she said, "to escape."

She threw her cigarette down on the pavement and stomped on it.

"Escape what?" I asked.

"My husband, Pat, is losing his mind. He has supranuclear palsy with dementia."

She said that her artist husband, once a pro boxer, had turned the mattress over on top of her, and he imagined that parties were going on in the living room when no one was there. And then, saying she should go inside to the show, my father's eldest cousin left me. Even though she meant nothing to me, I would remember our first real meeting perfectly.

* * *

Four years after the apparition of Charlotte outside my father's show, I would attend my own event at that same House of Books. I was still a doctoral student in English, teaching composition, but on this Thanksgiving weekend in 1985, I would sign my new book at the bookstore.

Orlando Slocum—The Story of a Young Artist was my humorous satire, a series of etchings with words, in which a young artist imitates great artists before realizing that his off-hand doodles are his best work. My mother, more ambitious than my father, had established her own small publishing venture, Truax Press; and after publishing a couple of her own projects, she published my little book.

Mid-Sunday before my book signing, my family sat in the living room of the remodeled saltbox farmhouse. Outside a breeze rippled high hay in the long field, an effect like ocean waves that my mother fell in love with back in 1960 when my parents bought the property. My father; my older sister, Beta, and her husband, Charles; and my younger sister, Suzanne, looked up as my mother ushered in a surprise guest who had arrived overnight. Charlotte had slept late in my father's studio and so was only now making her entrance. I wasn't interested in her at all, and only thought, *Here comes that weird old relic.*

Charlotte leaned forward on the couch, her legs jumpy, her red pumps sliding on the wide wooden floorboards. Just below her knees, visible white elastic bands held up her short stockings, which offended me for some reason. My mother, acting the master of ceremonies, treated the guest like a celebrity, reminding us that Charlotte's family, the Churches, had created the venerable Arm & Hammer Baking Soda company.

My mother brought the old woman a martini, and Charlotte started to talk. Everyone listened, even my father, holding a newspaper in his comfortable chair.

"Four horses in your field *watched me dress* this morning through the glass doors," she said, her face lighting up.

"Why shouldn't they?" said my mother. "You are a striking woman."

Lifting her martini, Charlotte splashed some on the floor. "Ha! I *thought* the horses wanted to see me, but a girl came to skim the ice off their trough—they only wanted their water, not interested in me at all."

This old lady talks too much, was my thought.

Three hours later people crowded into the bookstore as I signed my book. At first I felt a rush of accomplishment. But the surge of signings soon ended. I saw that the only people still in the place were family and friends, and my mood changed.

But my mother, with a group by the door, was undaunted, still trying to beat the drum of my success. Wearing her red and orange silk dress from her trip to China, she proclaimed to Bob Clark, a local composer, "Peter's book is witty and light. Art doesn't have to be serious to be great."

"Like a minor Chopin piece?" asked Bob.

"Chopin is never minor," my mother said.

Bob commented to my father, "Nick, your wife is Kent's pre-eminent aesthetician."

"We really want more people," my mother declared. And she took Bob's arm to go outside to lure more people in. And within minutes, having charmed several strangers, she steered them inside and toward me. But my attitude had gone sour, one of my black moods overtaking me: If I had any real talent, I would not need my strong-willed mother to publish me. It might as well have been a vanity press.

My mood would have grown even blacker, but a surprise distracted me when a tall man in a formal suit came in the door.

He had told me he would try to attend, but I'd doubted he would, because he had never been to this town before. The importance of this man was known only to my family. He was Doctor John P., the family psychoanalyst. Over the last two decades, in Manhattan, he had analyzed every member of my family but Suzanne—my father and my mother, Beta and Charles, and me. But, unlike with the others, he had become a close friend of mine. He came for my sake, so his presence was a feather in my cap.

His tailored European suit of gray-green made him look like a character out of Kafka's *The Trial*, overdressed for the country. But at six-foot-two, with a massive brow, even in his sixties he still cut an impressive figure.

He shook my hand. "I told you I wouldn't miss it for the world."

My mother was taken completely by surprise. My parents had originally suggested I see the Doctor for sessions after I graduated from college, but they knew him only as an analyst. Since he used a cane and suffered from sciatica, my mother ushered him to the only bench in the place, where old Charlotte happened to be sitting.

I went to get some wine for the Doctor, but I paused before bringing it back, overhearing their conversation. I didn't know it at the time, but the two most important people of my adult life—the Doctor, from the past, and Charlotte, in the future—were already bumping heads.

"Peter's mother said you've led a fascinating life, Charlotte," said the Doctor.

"I *still am* leading a fascinating life," she replied.

"I'm hard of hearing, sorry." He tapped a tiny microphone he wore.

"I hear perfectly," she said.

He gestured toward prints from my book on the wall. "Peter's sketches for his book are good."

"They're not sketches," Charlotte said. "They're *etchings!*"

"I know nothing about art."

"You certainly don't."

"I used to play the piano, Charlotte, but when my sister died, I couldn't keep the small Steinway. Truth told, I miss my sister's companionship. I often wish I'd never left Switzerland."

"Whoever said life was easy," said Charlotte. "Switzerland reminds me of lederhosen. My first husband wore them when he hiked from Switzerland to meet me in Venice."

I was struck by how unsure of himself, almost maudlin, the Doctor sounded in the presence of this elderly woman. In the city I'd had countless dinners out with him, just the two of us, but I seldom saw how he behaved socially.

Soon the book signing was over.

* * *

The next morning Suzanne and I sat side by side on the train back to Manhattan, and facing us was Charlotte, also returning to the city. Her knees almost touched mine. I looked out the window, trying to ignore her.

"Your book is great," she told me. "I love it."

Still in the mood of feeling my book was worthless, I wasn't about to be conned into thinking it was good.

"Openings are always awful," she commiserated.

I didn't say a word.

But Suzanne encouraged Charlotte to talk about anything or everything.

She said that her husband Pat got publicity for his openings because he had been a boxer, that newspaper photos showed his boxing glove holding paint brushes. A poor boy from Ireland, Pat Collins had joined the IRA at fifteen before he hired out on an Icelandic fishing trawler. To support himself while he painted in New York, he was a hod carrier, sandhog, carpenter, bouncer, and TV wrestling referee. In a Washington demonstration by WPA artists, Pat had snatched a cigarette out of Jackson Pollock's cynical mouth.

I didn't want to hear about Pat's exploits. Being a competitive type of person, constantly comparing myself with others, it only made me feel worse.

Next Charlotte talked about her first husband, Bunny Schroeder, a brilliant writer who, during the Depression, landed a job at *Time* magazine, where he invented the magazine's first-ever art column. Charlotte traveled the world with Bunny the journalist, making friends with the likes of John Dos Passos, Hemingway, and Alexander Calder.

Suzanne, all ears, asked Charlotte to tell us about our father, her cousin, since he rarely talked about his early life.

"Oh, Nick was an odd duck. He didn't take to riding horses the way his father wanted him to."

My grandfather, who was called Pecks, had been a domineering, macho Master of Fox Hounds in Michigan. I remembered him from our only trip out there when I was little. Pecks took me riding, galloping ahead of me on his favorite mount, Black Rock, while I barely stayed on my horse behind him.

Charlotte said, "I watched your father ride around and around on a white pony when he was five. Poor Nicky kept asking, 'Can I get off now? Can I get off now?'"

The light dimmed as our train moved underground to Grand Central. Since I'd not said a word in an hour, Charlotte reached out and touched my knee, and said, "Pecks *didn't talk*, either. Just like you. He didn't say a word until he was four. People thought he couldn't speak, until one day he said, '*Peck's Bad Boy*,' the famous book title. That's how he got his nickname."

I'd heard enough. I said, "Charlotte, you talk *too much*."

She blinked hard and drew up her knees. Suzanne nudged me, meaning that I'd been cruel. As the train came to a stop, Charlotte spoke to Suzanne, mentioning that she had paintings in her apartment that she wanted to rehang, and that she could use some help.

By then I'd realized that I'd taken out my black book-signing mood on an innocent old woman.

"I'm sorry, Charlotte," I apologized. "I didn't mean what I said."

"Yes, you did!" she shot back.

She stepped into the aisle. "I was sixteen when your grandfather told me the exact same thing—that I talk too much. Do you know what I told him? That *I like to talk!*" She pointed her finger at me. "You're like Pecks, and your *father*, too, in a different way."

Charlotte lifted her small suitcase, said goodbye to Suzanne, and left the train.

I was stunned. I didn't mind being compared to manly Pecks, but I did to my father, whose detached coolness I hated.

Suzanne handed me a slip of paper on which she'd written Charlotte's phone number. She suggested I might make amends by helping Charlotte rehang her paintings. I might. But if I did, my real purpose would be to prove that I wasn't like my father.

* * *

The evening after the train ride, I stared out my West Side fifth- floor apartment window at the brownstones across 85th Street, so close that they resembled a stage set, with other people's lives played out through their windows. I'd seen a chubby, nervous woman pace back and forth for hours. A beefy man lifted weights. One night, a few months ago, a slender, elegant young woman had set up a large mirror against her back bedroom wall, opened a bottle of wine, and then danced in her slip. She was dancing for me, using the mirror so I could see her better. But when she opened her window and looked straight at me, I froze, too timid to shout a greeting to her.

I'd had my share of girlfriends, but I also endured long periods without anyone. And I was in one of those lonely times now.

My working life was a patchwork of small potatoes and big hopes. On my desk lay a stack of student essays from the two composition courses I taught at Brooklyn Polytechnic. On my walls were a dozen paintings looking for a show someday, and portraits of models done at the Art Students League, practice before starting a portrait business. Rather than ask my father for support, I wanted to make it on my own.

But I'd had trouble finding my niche in the real world of work ever since I graduated, cum laude, from Beloit College. During college, I had done typical '60s things—smoked dope, lived briefly like a hippie in San Francisco, had girlfriends. But I stumbled coming out of the gate after graduation. I lacked confidence. Even if I could do something well, my self-esteem drained out of me like water from a pail with a hole in it.

2

A Kiss That Changed Everything

I hadn't forgotten Charlotte's accusations on the train, but I did not call her for two months. In the meantime, in January 1986, my mother invited me for a lunch in the city. She was in town seeing an editor at Harper and Row about her paperback version of an elaborate portfolio she'd created combining famous Chinese poems, calligraphy, and her own drawings.

We sat down in Isle of Capri, her favorite East Side restaurant.

"Good news," she said. "I wrote to the Morgan Library about your *Orlando* book, and they'll buy eight copies for their bookstore."

I nodded, surprised that the Morgan was interested.

"But that's not why I want to talk," my mother said. Her face turned mournful, her square jaw tightened under her prominent cheekbones. "I have something on my mind. If I am ever connected to a machine in a hospital, I don't want to be kept alive that way."

Her words were so unexpected that I almost didn't take them in. She was in good health. She had high blood pressure but took medication for that. So I took what she said in the spirit of her always having been a dramatist, freighting life with extra meaning. One reason that our family had lived in Athens for a year, my eighth-grade year, had been her passion for ancient Greek drama, sculpture, and the Acropolis.

She took another sip of her Manhattan.

"Another thing," said my mother, "Your father is trying very hard. I hope you will give him another chance."

This really did surprise me.

Her history had been more to complain about my father. From too early an age, I'd heard her excoriate him for being sexually cold and emotionally distant. And after he had shown real talent in early abstracted landscapes, his painting had stopped developing. My mother, when I was ten, had told me that he would one day "become one of the world's ten best painters." That was impossible, so how was he improving?

"Your father is changing," she said now. "And he wants to know you better."

"He's had plenty of chances," I said.

Over dessert she handed me a gift: a collage she'd pasted together with a photo of her father, Eli, at its center and four smaller pictures of me, aged about six or seven, around him. This grandfather had died before my memory began. Looking now, I saw a resemblance between Eli's shy, deep-set eyes and my own.

Before we left the restaurant, my mother asked if I had contacted Charlotte.

* * *

The next day, I made the call, offering to rehang Charlotte's paintings. Her voice sounded softer, less aggressive than on the train. She invited me to her apartment.

The following afternoon, I walked through Central Park, then east on 68th Street until I reached the polished brass of the maroon awning, number 333. The brick of the building was almost entirely covered in ivy. The doorman directed me across a checkerboard marble floor to the rosewood-paneled elevator. This was definitely "old New York." I got off on the thirteenth floor—the number that newer buildings often skip.

I knocked on her door. Charlotte, wearing a white dress with black-striped zebras running across it, put out her hand and, with a surprisingly strong grip, drew me inside.

"I am not a good housekeeper, I am bohemian," she said, as she started me on a tour of her spacious apartment. The dark green anteroom led into a long, white living room with different styles of furniture: a modern black couch, an ancient chair with sheep's head arms, an Italian side table, a leather-covered oval desk, an art nouveau lamp. There was a working fireplace. The worn zebra rug, she said, was courtesy of her Aunt Charlotte's good aim while on a safari in Africa with Uncle Charlie.

I noticed peeling paint on the ceiling above the north windows. The apartment was impressive but neglected, probably since husband Pat's death. But I liked the warm and wittily eclectic atmosphere.

Every painting in the living room was by Pat, including a portrait of Charlotte above the fireplace. "It took him seven years to finish it, in the '40s," she said. In the painting she was sitting on a rooftop, above the life of the city, holding an empty martini glass at an angle. In a gown of red and blue stripes, with her clear, high forehead, intense brown eyes, and long, glossy brown hair, she looked more like thirty than nearly fifty. But her expression was slightly forlorn, as though she'd grown tired of modeling for Pat.

Next Charlotte showed me her Venetian-red library and dining room. A sixteenth-century map of Venice hung next to shelves of Venetian glass. She pointed out her two favorite book collections: Hemingway, and children's books illustrated by Edmund Dulac. On the dining room table was a two-tailed mermaid sculpture Bunny had purchased for her in Venice.

Down the hallway to the bedrooms was an impressionist painting, by Charlotte's father, of their family mansion in New Rochelle. "Father exaggerated the height of the columns to make Mother happy," Charlotte said. "As you know, your grandfather Pecks's two sisters married two brothers—my father and my uncle. But Uncle Charlie and Aunt Charlotte never had children. I was the first-born for all of them. We all lived together, great friends." Her face lit up with remembered joy. "Ha! I felt like I had *four* parents."

I was starting to see elderly Charlotte as an individual, not as the cliché I'd thought she was. She didn't seem to be holding my rudeness on the train against me now. It occurred to me that she was lonely. Her enthusiasm in giving me the tour suggested she hadn't had many guests since Pat's death.

She showed me a small oil painting of an eggplant by a friend of hers, Bradley Tomlin, whose later large abstractions I'd seen at the Metropolitan Museum.

"It's getting late," I said. "We'd better do the paintings."

I used a stepladder to take down one of Pat's vertical, surreal cityscapes, in which grotesque, humorous little figures decorated the metropolis. A man pulled a donkey up a fire escape; a woman with breasts in back and buttocks in front stood in a window. This bigger picture would trade places with a smaller one, in which first husband Bunny was depicted as a mouse climbing up a water pitcher.

The larger painting left a brighter space on the wall that was too big for the smaller painting to cover—that's how long the paintings had hung in their places as the white paint around them faded.

After that, I rewired a painting directly over Charlotte's bed, for safety's sake. She looked up at me on the ladder. "It's wonderful to have a big, strong man around."

Being a short and never particularly "handy" man, I enjoyed the compliment.

Charlotte suggested we celebrate work done by having martinis, but I explained that I had too many student essays to correct for teaching the next morning. Do you like to eat lobster, she asked. Yes, I did. Then when I had the time, she would take me to her favorite restaurant for lobsters, just around the corner.

As I left, she whispered, "You can tell me if I talk too much."

* * *

Two nights later I escorted Charlotte to The Lobster, named for its specialty. I was surprised by how much I'd looked forward to this, but I felt a bit on my guard. Somehow I didn't think I should enjoy too much going out with an elderly woman. I was only doing Charlotte a favor.

"Mrs. Collins," said the maître d', "it's wonderful to see you again. How have you been?"

"Perfectly fine."

Once we were seated, Charlotte whispered, "That maître d' is a shit. After Pat died, I came here alone, and he stuck me by the kitchen door."

We ordered gin martinis and twin lobsters.

Charlotte told me that after Pat's death, unable to sleep at night, she had read countless crime novels. Finally she dared go to The Lobster, by herself. "But I drank too much and fell off my chair, banging my head. That horrible maître d' wanted me *out the door* immediately. He didn't do one thing to help me, even though my head was *bleeding*. Thank God a total stranger outside, a nice black man, gave me his arm and walked me home."

Charlotte tore into her soft-shelled lobster, liquid spilling all over her fingers. I liked her unselfconscious style. On my second martini, I was feeling comfortable.

"I have a temper," she suddenly confided. "My worst deadly sins are anger and jealousy. I once hit Bunny over the head with a phone, because he wanted to desert me to go out with another woman to a party." I had seen the probable weapon in Charlotte's kitchen, a heavy old rotary phone.

"What's your worst deadly sin?" she asked me.

"Envy," I admitted.

I was thinking that I liked the seven deadly sins because they seemed less abstract and bloodless than modern psychological categories. My family was steeped in psychoanalysis, analyzing life constantly. Whereas, I was noticing, Charlotte seemed to live her life more naturally. She simply lived.

Now on my third martini, I contentedly listened to Charlotte tell a story from before World War I. At the Ziegfeld Midnight Frolic at the Amsterdam Theater, she and her parents sat in the front row as pretty chorus girls skated an arm's length away, racing by in sparkly dresses and carrying umbrellas with tinsel and glass raindrops. Charlotte waved her finger. "Father suddenly jumped up and ran onto the ice after one of the girls!"

"Really?"

"Mother had a fit. She thought Father would someday fall in love with a chorus girl and run off, but not so soon."

"Was he . . .?"

"No. Father's pince-nez was caught on a girl's umbrella, so he had to run to get them back."

We had desserts of crème brulée. That's when I shared some news about my former analyst. He'd called me after the signing, saying that in driving home afterward, he had skidded on an oil slick and totaled his car.

"Good!" said Charlotte.

"Fortunately he wasn't injured."

"Too bad. What a horrible man. All he did was complain about his life. How could he possibly help anyone else?"

Her dismissal of the Doctor stung. I felt compelled to defend him. I extolled his credentials: he'd known Jung, been analyzed by Jung's mistress, and spoke fluent German. When only in his twenties, I said, he had been assigned as a postwar governor for the Allies in Germany. I added that he was a believer in Jewish culture and wisdom, often quoting Rabbi Hillel.

Charlotte did not look impressed.

I shared with her that my mother was Jewish, even if her family had adopted Christian Science. I told her that I'd heard how my parents' two families, Jewish Christian Scientists and Catholic, had each thought themselves better than the other family.

"I know all that," said Charlotte, "I saw it. I once lent the key to my own apartment to your parents, before they married, so they could be together. It took guts for your parents to elope."

Elope? They'd never told me.

Charlotte frowned. "It's hard to be different. When I was in the Red Cross during World War II, my boss called me the 'rich bitch from uptown' just because I came from money."

Charlotte paid for our dinner. Outside, she invited me back to her apartment for a nightcap. How could I say no? It was my duty. Truth was, I wanted to.

High on drink, I felt good. I remembered a '40s movie, *The Thin Man*, and imagined Charlotte being like that, a "fast-talking dame" like Myrna Loy or Bette Davis. Smart, animated, and attractive.

Ascending in the elevator, I thought how much Charlotte's long perspective outreached even my parents' lives. She knew life before World War I, before my parents were born. Charlotte offered a peek through a magic keyhole in time. Incredibly, as she had mentioned, Charlotte had attended my own grandfather Pecks's wedding. It seemed impossible, except that she was a full seventeen years older than my father.

In her kitchen she made us martinis before we sat on the black Naugahyde couch.

She was oddly quiet, as though for once not sure what to say, before she talked. "I never told this to anyone except Pat, but something terrible happened to me when I was thirty-one." Charlotte paused to light up a Camel. "I was still a virgin, ten years married to Bunny. I was staying at my parents' place on Long Island, when Uncle Pecks visited, and invited me out for a drive."

A virgin after how long married? Had I heard that right?

"Pecks drove us down a long country road, and parked. He said that he'd busted his Uncle Giles's will. Not just for himself, he said, but for me, too, so I'd get my trust money outright."

I could appreciate that. My father had a trust but couldn't touch its capital. He was like a kid on a permanent allowance.

Charlotte wrung her hands. "Pecks said I should be grateful. Then he climbed on top of me, *jumped on me* for sex. He was built like a jockey, strong for a small man."

I'd heard Pecks chased women, but his niece?

"Somehow I pushed him off." Charlotte dabbed her eyes with a Kleenex. "I felt so ashamed, like I'd been raped."

I was amazed she was telling me this. But whatever I could say to comfort her was fifty years too late.

Charlotte had dropped her lit cigarette. To pick it up for her, I shifted closer on the couch. Recomposing herself, under better control, she said,

"When I was young, I don't know why, I was afraid of sex. Some people are just like that. Bunny was a wonderful travel companion, but more interested in men, so when I finally asked him for sex, he refused."

I rarely smoked, but I asked if I could have one of hers. Possibly I had never heard another human being tell me so much about themselves in so short a time. When Charlotte opened up about herself, wow, she really opened up.

"Now I'm old!" she said, angry. Then, sadly, "Who could I possibly get now?"

I was struck by her honesty. I had known enough loneliness myself to relate to hers. It sounds corny, but Charlotte's distress went straight to my heart.

"You could get somebody," I said.

She raised her hands to primp her smooth white hair, which had a perfect lilt at the nape of her neck. It was such a classic feminine gesture. She looked at me. "I'm sorry, on the train, that I said you're like Pecks or your father. You're not."

I'm not sure how to tell what happened next. Maybe I'm afraid to tell. She was so attractive for her age, and her energy felt young. It was a moment outside of time, and I lived in that moment. Leaning close, I kissed her on her lips, and she kissed back. Her mouth was soft and warm, fresh as any younger woman's. Our hands touched. The only odd thing about the moment was that it did not feel odd. Her hand stroked mine.

When we stopped kissing, Charlotte's gray eyes were bright. For me, there was nothing premeditated here at all, it just happened. Only much later would I know that ours was a once-in-a-lifetime kiss, a little crazy but transcendent, and that it changed everything.

Without a word, we stood and went down the hallway to her bedroom. In the glow from city lights through the window, we lay down on her narrow bed, and gently touched each other. Make no mistake, by this time I was very sexually aroused. And Charlotte liked it. Off came our clothes. My memory, from drink, perhaps, is a little hazy, but I was wide awake at the time, and soon, from her touch, I climaxed. And Charlotte hugged me.

I must have drifted into sleep, because I woke feeling I should go home to my own bed. I didn't want to spend the whole night. Maybe I was embarrassed by what had happened. Charlotte seemed to understand. I dressed. In her robe she walked me to her apartment door, where she asked when she might see me again. I don't remember giving her any answer.

* * *

Back in my apartment, I slept immediately. No doubt, if I'd woken up slowly the next morning, I'd have sorted through the details of my surprising time with Charlotte. But it was my phone ringing at six AM that woke me.

It was my father.

"I have bad news," he said. "Your mother is in Hartford Hospital. She's had a cerebral hemorrhage. It doesn't look good." He said that in the evening she'd complained of a terrible headache and gone upstairs, and then he'd found her unconscious. She was airlifted to Hartford, where the doctors said an aneurysm had burst, seeping blood between her brain and skull.

My father said to call my sister Suzanne.

Within a couple of hours, Suzanne and I were on a bus to Hartford, holding hands, wondering how bad it must be. When we arrived at the hospital, we were told that our mother was brain dead. Her talk with me at our recent lunch had turned out to be a premonition, because only a machine kept her breathing. The only good thing was that the decision to take her off the machine was not in itself hard; it was only about when exactly to say goodbye.

* * *

My father, sisters, Charles, and I sat with the director of the Hartford funeral parlor that took my mother's body. The director said he had to ask us a few "necessary questions."

"You've chosen cremation?"

"Yes," said my father.

"What was the deceased's place of birth?"

"Cambridge, Massachusetts," my father said.

"Her age?"

"Sixty-five," said Suzanne.

"Do I understand correctly that you don't want a service here? We can accommodate you. We have . . ."

"No," said my father. "It will be at our house in Kent."

The director made a note on his pad.

"We have several choices for urns. We have brass."

"The simplest possible," said my father.

"The simplest would be plastic," said the director.

"Fine," said my father.

The director skipped a beat for a moment, but his expression did not change. The conversation started to feel like a play script in which only we, the family, knew the right lines.

"Plastic's not a sign of disrespect," I told the director. "We're liberals."

"To us," said Suzanne, "plastic is even *better* than brass."

The bereaved smiled at each other. The mood was so intense that something had to give, and it took the form of giddy humor.

"We should get two," Beta, a rational history professor, suggested. "One should be brass, to give to Uncle Howard."

My mother's lone surviving brother had established a family plot on Cape Cod.

"One brass, one plastic urn, then," said the director. "Ashes equally divided between them?"

"Correct," said my father, frowning, about to lose his patience. "Let's get this *done*, for God's sake! What other information could you possibly need?"

"Sorry, sir. Just two more questions. Is Mrs. Nichols wearing anything like a hearing aid? Anything that could explode in the kiln?"

"No," my father said.

The director made a check on his form.

"Was Mrs. Nichols a veteran?"

"Of *what?*" asked my father incredulously.

We all glanced at each other.

"Of the armed forces."

We looked back and forth at each other, laughing again.

"A veteran only of life," said Beta dryly. "Not of the military."

"I can see none of you have lost your sense of humor," said the director.

But of course the humor was a necessary release. Suzanne had become almost hysterical at the hospital, when, after she'd asked the staff to wait, they'd turned off the breathing machine when she was not in the room. Later that night, in a motel room she shared with her boyfriend, Steve, Suzanne saw my mother's spirit in the form of an orange light hovering in the air above. Seeing that light would be the start of a long spiritual quest for her. Whereas Beta and I would react similarly, breaking out in sudden sobs together, as though we were linked. My father, showing less overt feeling, was mostly quiet.

That weekend we had a service at the house in Kent. People simply spoke or read something, and my mother's friend Louise played her violin. There was no priest or religious authority. I did a small oil portrait of my mother and showed it to everyone.

For a few days, we were all together as a family. My father seemed, to me, like just another abandoned sibling. I imagined that we were survivors in a small boat in a storm, riding a swell so vast that all normal reference points were gone.

The night after the service, I dreamt that my family was sitting around a table in a room when the door opened, and my mother came in to say goodbye. It seemed such a healthy dream that I imagined I was accepting her death.

It was only later that I had the presence of mind to reflect on the extraordinary coincidence: my mother's brain hemorrhage had happened the same night that I had gone to Charlotte's bedroom. Of course the two events had nothing to do with each other. I was a skeptic and a believer in reason. But I still found myself wondering: Had some kind of knowledge of my mother's dying flowed from my mother to me, unconsciously, like blood over space, that night, drawing me toward an older woman? Or, conversely, had knowledge of my going to bed with Charlotte, forty-seven years older than I, flowed toward my mother and touched off a deadly headache?

I didn't believe that. Did I?

Whatever happened, it wouldn't be until years later that I would wonder whether, if my mother had lived, I would have felt constrained in knowing Charlotte. Would my mother's presence have made me embarrassed to be so intimate with Charlotte? Would my mother's sharp intuition have discovered what was going on?

But I'm getting ahead of myself. I'll never know.

3

Country Charlotte

Back in New York, I saw Charlotte only occasionally, and not in a bedroom. Once I had dinner out with her and an elderly couple she knew, with whom it was easy for me to play the role of the young cousin-once-removed. As spring approached, Charlotte, as always, planned to spend her summer in Woodstock, New York, in the house that she and Pat had bought in 1949 (the year I was born). Pat had been a part of that town's art community, which flourished long before the famous '60s concert— actually held in nearby Bethel— that took its name from Woodstock.

I had no summer teaching. I'd always been close to my sister Suzanne, who'd decided to stay for the summer with my father, and still in the mood of family mourning, I sublet my apartment so that I could also stay in Kent. Suzanne's bubbly warmth filled the space between my father and me, making it easier for us to live in the same house.

While there, I painted in my mother's studio. I used old family photographs, especially of children, to focus on a variety of facial expressions: sadness, joy, loneliness, anger, ambivalence. No doubt it was a way to connect to my own emotions. One painting was of myself at about a year old, deliriously happy and holding a paintbrush; but my baby self was imprisoned inside a giant, expressionless male skull. Another painting was of two little boys on an island in Maine, exploring shore rocks outside the summer house my father still owned. One boy was older and wiser, the other wide-eyed and vulnerable: two sides of myself.

Then a different kind of painting emerged. I created a simulacrum person, a hollow figure whose head was left open from behind. The point of view was as though looking out through the eyes of the empty, concave, masklike head. I was trying to paint consciousness. I only half-realized that the emptiness of those heads, like dug-out pumpkins with holes for eyes, expressed a deep emptiness in myself.

While I painted, Suzanne was keeping in close touch with Charlotte. My sister found her life stories so intriguing that each week she drove an hour and a half to Woodstock to help Charlotte speak her memoirs. Suzanne returned with tape-recorded interviews to transcribe onto paper.

I wasn't thinking much about Charlotte. I'd met twenty-six-year-old Alexis, a friend of Suzanne's. Taller than I, with long, blond hair, she was statuesque and sexy. I invited her to picnic beside the Housatonic River, which flowed through Kent. We had wine and cheese on a small stretch of sand. In my old room at the house, we went to bed. But in the middle of sex, the experience felt oddly empty to me. It was as though I could sense no definite center, no core, in Alexis. Then, after a visit to her parents' house—where I felt too shy, and old, to pal around with Alex and a girlfriend of hers—our short affair ended.

Then I thought of Charlotte. If anyone had a definite center, it was Charlotte. Suddenly I knew I wanted to go to Woodstock.

I had a fear of driving to new places, but armed with Suzanne's directions, in my mother's old car, I drove the serpentine country roads, then over the long expanse of the Kingston-Rhinecliff Bridge across the Hudson River. I could see, in pale, atmospheric perspective, the mountains beyond Woodstock. A half hour later I turned left up little Hillman Road and left again down Charlotte's driveway.

She sat waiting for me on a wrought-iron bench in the recessed entrance to her house. She wore her Venetian gondolier's hat, a denim jacket, blue jeans, and moccasins—Charlotte in country mode.

She pointed up in the air. "This giant spruce in the turnaround has *two* tops because a lightning bolt struck it way up there, and two tops grew back. The lightning *cracked* the stone step you're standing on."

Inside the front door, the hall led both left and right to symmetrical, high-ceilinged rooms whose windows started five feet from the floor. Charlotte said, "Those are artist's windows, high so no one outside can see a naked model inside."

The rest of the house was what she called "jerrybuilt"—small, narrow rooms added on at right angles. Beyond Charlotte's bedroom, like walking through a tunnel, was a bathroom and then a tiny library containing a hand-winder Victrola and a bed. That would be my room.

Charlotte served us martinis and smoked salmon out on the crescent-shaped stone patio behind the house. A froth of high Queen Anne's lace flowers showed white against the surrounding deep woods. The back outside wall of the house was painted a bright pink, unlike the white of the rest of house. Charlotte's trusty handyman, John, an Englishman who'd been the lone survivor of a World War I bomb demolition team, did painting and trimmed bushes and raked the driveway for her. He also drove her into town so she could stock up on groceries.

"You're painting, I hear from Suzanne," said Charlotte.

I described my paintings.

"You should have a show." Then she raised a hand to her ear. "Listen, I hear a wood thrush."

I heard liquid notes in descending sets of three.

For the first time I was with country Charlotte, lover of nature. And right away I learned how much she liked to talk about it. Her comments went on and on.

"Pat and I gave copies of *Silent Spring* to all our neighbors in the '60s, but they paid no attention. Ah, the poor birds.

"Once I thought I saw a small bear climb that mulberry tree there. But it was a big *raccoon!* Everybody says raccoons don't climb, but they do.

"Pat found a garter snake with a gash in it. Pat put him on the ironing board to sew him up with needle and thread, and the snake didn't move a muscle, and Pat saved him.

"Those trees over there are oaks, those there are spruce. That's a snowball bush with its petals turning pink."

Listening, I felt slightly ashamed. I'd grown up in the country, but my parents and I only painted nature. We understood almost nothing about it. In contrast, Charlotte's father and uncle were naturalists. Her father traveled far and wide collecting butterflies, and he was one of the first to go down in his friend William Beebe's famous bathysphere, after which he painted fish on his daughter Charlotte's bedroom wall. Her Uncle Charlie and Aunt Charlotte hunted lions and zebras on safari in Africa, and moose in Canada.

After a dinner of filet mignon, red potatoes, and baby lima beans, we went into the library to wind up the Victrola and play thick old 33 rpm records: Cole Porter, the Mills Brothers, Bix Beiderbecke. Charlotte also loved rock 'n' roll, particularly Elvis, which she listened to on her kitchen radio.

It was late, bedtime. In my room, I couldn't quite settle down, and I wondered how Charlotte felt about the sex we'd once had. The more I remembered and thought about it, the more aroused I became. Carefully holding my robe front out to hide how turned on I was, I stepped through the bathroom between us and knocked on her door.

"Come in," she called. She lifted the sheet for me to slide in beside her. "So you still like the old lady."

I didn't stop to think about age or what was considered acceptable behavior in the "normal" world. We made love side-by-side until I dared to lift myself over her on my hands and knees, careful not to put my full weight on her. Gently I moved, sliding, skin to skin, until I came, and she hugged me.

Fortunately, like me, Charlotte preferred to go to sleep alone. A light sleeper, I'd had experiences with women who felt they must sleep beside, or entangled with, a man. Mercifully, Charlotte shared my conviction that sleeping arrangements have nothing necessarily to do with intimacy. We were both free to get a good night's sleep, separately, in our own beds.

The next morning Charlotte stood at the woods' edge waving goodbye as I drove down Hillman Road. I would visit her several more times that summer. Whatever Suzanne or my father thought about my staying with Charlotte, I knew that she wouldn't divulge our secret.

4

Portrait of the Analyst

The hiatus in Kent over, I resumed my life in the city. As was my habit, I got together with Doctor John P., my former psychoanalyst. Typically we met for dinner at a restaurant, but on this occasion he invited me to his office, saying he had a surprise for me.

His building on Park Avenue and 39th Street had a gingerbread look, mustard-colored. As usual, I nodded at the doorman and took the elevator to the twelfth floor. His door was ajar for me, kept open by a little yellow rubber triangle. I immediately saw, sitting in the middle of the one-room apartment, a slender wooden crate about three feet high. Without a word, the Doctor unscrewed several nuts from the wood, and lifted out a painting. It was a portrait of the Doctor by another former patient, a wealthy gay artist whom I'd met, named Bradley Phillips.

The likeness, in pastel under glass, was perfect. The Doctor sat at his desk with a pen poised, writing a note. Behind reflecting bifocals, his eyes suggested deep thought. On shelves beyond the Doctor were books by Szasz, Aristotle, Kant, all rendered in impressive detail. On the desk were little talismans—gifts from "graduated" patients: a plastic swimmer, a coiled brass salamander, a tiny ship-in-a-bottle.

But the portrait looked soulless—a cliché, not the man I knew better.

"A friend of Bradley's calls it an icon of the psychoanalyst," said the Doctor. "He offered me twenty-five thousand dollars for it." He laughed bitterly.

"What's funny?"

"Bradley gave it to me on condition that I never sell it."

I understood. I knew the Doctor was down to two or three patients, and that he owed thousands on his credit cards. He was living proof that a Park Avenue analyst could be a financial disaster. He was old school, believing in traditional analysis, at least three times a week, scoffing at mere once-a-week therapy. But he wasn't good at making connections to garner new patients.

"When I die," he said somberly, "I want you to have Brad's portrait of me."

We walked to a reasonably priced Italian restaurant, where we ordered a carafe of wine, lasagna for him, linguini a la vongola for me. I'd already told him about visiting Charlotte in Woodstock. Now, wine in hand, he said, "The old woman, what's her name, she could help you with art connections, and money. She's rich, isn't she?"

"Her name's Charlotte, and she's a real friend."

"A better friend than me?" he smiled. "Don't worry, Peter, I know you love me, even if you sometimes hate me."

At the moment, there was no point getting into a debate about the nature of our friendship.

We had a long history, the Doctor and I. The word *friend* had a special meaning between us, because he'd stressed it so much back when our relationship had changed. But he was the only person I had told about my closeness with Charlotte. Despite our differences, he remained an authority figure for me.

As we finished our dinner, I turned the conversation to other things, asking whether Bradley was up for a show of his paintings and whether the Doctor had been to the Jung Society lately, where occasionally he used to find new patients.

Outside the restaurant, we shook hands, and I watched him cross the street to buy a lottery ticket and a bottle of bourbon to get him through the night. I felt sorry for him but was still annoyed at his cavalier disrespect for Charlotte. I walked west to catch a bus uptown to my apartment.

On the bus, the Doctor's claim that I loved him reverberated in my mind. In order to explain the situation, I have to go back more than a dozen years, to the time after my graduation from college in 1971.

For my first real jobs, I worked in a Manhattan public-relations company mailroom and then as a "go-fer" trainee in a print advertising studio. Because I made little money, I accepted a stipend from my father to pay for my analysis with the Doctor, whom my parents had recommended.

In New York, at first, for over a year, I had a wonderful girlfriend named Arvella, a black secretary with two small children. But then she landed a scholarship to a Midwestern college and moved away, leaving me feeling lonely in the big city.

Meanwhile, I was nervously waiting to be inducted into the army, having gotten a low number, 12, in the Vietnam War draft. I asked the Doctor to write a letter to my draft board so that my "character neurosis" could keep me out of the army. I was against the war, but I felt cowardly avoiding the draft, and ashamed that my strategy worked.

It is difficult to know if you've chosen the right analyst when you are unsure of yourself in the first place. The Doctor seemed to me to be arrogant, even while, at the same time, there was an aroma of weakness about him, an odd hint of obsequiousness, as though he himself were desperate in the world. I simply wasn't quite comfortable with him.

So I told him that I would end my analysis.

That's when the Doctor changed everything by making a surprising suggestion. After saying that I was his most talented patient, since I could both paint and write, he offered to see me for free. Of course I felt complimented when, summing up his proposal, he said he was offering me his "friendship."

This appealed to my vanity, and my curiosity. Imagine knowing the "family analyst" far better than either of my parents, former patients, ever could. So I accepted.

Soon he was taking me to dinners at good restaurants, where he always paid. He told me about his life, so it was a two-way street. I learned how he had worked at a munitions factory to put himself through college, had known Jung at his institute in Switzerland, and had been assigned as a postwar "governor" for the Allies in Germany, traveling from town to town attending democratic meetings.

And I learned that he was secretly gay. He had spoken about the essential bisexuality of all people, but that opinion had not affected me personally. But one day in his office, I mentioned that I had a bad case of "jock itch" that was a real annoyance. Saying that he had originally wanted to be a general practitioner, he suggested he take a look. I unzipped my pants. "Use the cream here, not here," he told me, before looking up at me with soulful eyes. "You have a beautiful penis."

I'll never understand completely why I let him give me blowjobs, but I did. For one thing, I got a hard-on. The Doctor had claimed that only a person who explored his bisexuality could fully develop as a human being. And at first it seemed relatively harmless, since he seemed to expect no active role for me. But I had no idea what I was getting myself into with the Doctor.

I began to realize how much he needed me. His only sexual partners, for years, had been patients or former patients, and now, in his sixties, he had no other "friend" besides me. Apparently he was incapable of taking the risk of meeting friends in the wider world. He was too frightened, or too proud, to take part in the new freedom being fought for by the gay community. He despised the word *gay*.

But he did care for me as a person, and I was grateful that, any time, night or day, I could talk with him about any problem.

But sexual contact with him made me increasingly uncomfortable. He must have sensed my reluctance, but that didn't stop him. An orgasm with him always held a sad, bitter undertone that depressed me. He would pathetically say that I was his last best friend, so I felt guilty pushing him away.

He kept raising the sexual ante, wanting me to participate actively. Twice he convinced me to let him visit my apartment, where I tried more complete sex with him.

Then, finally, I got angry.

At a restaurant one night, he insisted on paying the check before going home with me. I said no. I accused him of trying to *buy* friendship, and dropped two twenty-dollar bills on the table for my share of the bill, and left the restaurant alone.

The next week, in his office, he tried to give me the forty dollars. He tried to hug me into his hips. Impulsively, infuriated, I punched him in the stomach, hard enough to hurt. And that was it. He finally gave up. He never asked for sex again.

Oddly, because we'd gotten to know each other so well, we remained friends. But then it was more on my terms.

I had not been an innocent child when the sex began, but I had been a very naïve young adult. The irony of it was that I learned more from being involved with him and then getting myself out of the sexual situation than I ever did from the analysis. I learned how desperation like the Doctor's could lead one person to manipulate another. And if I ever had any doubts, I confirmed that I was not really bisexual but attracted only to females.

For better or worse, the Doctor and I had a bond, and we remained friends for more than a dozen years, until the time when I met Charlotte.

I got off my bus at 85th Street. Perhaps, in some way I would never understand, I depended on the Doctor still, but there was no point dwelling too much on the past.

5

Making a Living

With Charlotte back from Woodstock, I stayed overnight at her apartment at least once a week. We'd sometimes drink martinis and dine on smoked salmon or beluga caviar in her living room. Of course the food was a treat, but one evening a seemingly small gesture on her part impressed me. She said, "Go on—put your feet up on the table." It was her fine old glass-topped coffee table. Her invitation to do as she liked to do, feet up, helped me feel a part of her world. Charlotte had a way of bringing me upwards with her—rather than touching off my pattern of comparing myself with another.

I was working on my English doctorate, teaching composition at Brooklyn Polytechnic and tutoring at Manhattan Community College, in the shadow of the World Trade Center.

And I started doing quick portraits for money, specializing in pastels of babies and children. I'd always loved portraiture, as my mother had. Painting a portrait could be a wonderfully wordless, silent communion between artist and subject. I hoped it could still be that, even when done for money.

I helped a Mrs. Schwartz carry her baby Sam in his stroller up to my apartment. Sam, too little to stay still, bobbed his head and gyrated his arms like a tiny prizefighter, and then he fell asleep. I could have taken photos to help me finish, but I hated copying from photos. So I tried to imagine Baby Sam with his eyes open. Two hours later, checking my work in a mirror, I saw that my Sam resembled a prizefighter who'd lost: one eye was blackened with too much shadow, and one cheek was crimson and swollen out.

So I told Mrs. Schwartz that I would have to finish the portrait overnight and deliver it to her office in the morning. It took me another three hours.

At her office building, Mrs. Schwartz squinted at the portrait. "It is Sam, but doesn't his blanket look like a barrel? Like he's sitting in a barrel."

"I think it's wonderful," said the receptionist. "How much do you charge?"

"Fifty dollars."

A man in a suit said, "You'll never make a living at that price. Do you paint them for fun?"

The portrait was flawed, and I walked away feeling like I'd stolen fifty dollars. I should be thicker-skinned. It was becoming clear to me that a portraitist must also be a salesman. If a portrait wasn't your best, just take the money and run. No wonder most quick-portrait artists worked by formula, to avoid obvious mistakes. Stupid me, trying to do original work—art.

Charlotte understood. When I described the Baby Sam experience to her, she told me a story about her artist friend Bradley Tomlin. Before he became famous, he had tried to do her portrait, in Woodstock. He became so frustrated by his effort that he angrily tore up the portrait and fed it to his potbelly stove for heat. Like me, Charlotte disliked what she called "candy-box art," art that was facile and predictable.

But, art aside, I had a problem with feeling that I had earned a paycheck. It was a kind of blind spot about working for money at all. When I picked up my paychecks for teaching, the money seemed almost an abstraction, as though I could not have earned it. Maybe being raised in a family living on trusts, in which "art for art's sake" was the only reality, had spoiled me for mere work for dough. On the other hand, I knew I idealized the normal working world, as though I weren't competent enough for it.

At least teaching lent me some stature, since most students assumed that a teacher deserved respect. But there was one class that winter that did not go that way. We had read Sophocles's *Oedipus Rex*, and I used the ancient play for a class debate to help students learn how to write an argument essay. The play happened to have special meaning for me, because when I was only ten years old, my mother had forced me to read it. At the time she had been trying to correct my preference for reading only comic books. I barely understood a word of the play.

In Brooklyn I wrote on the blackboard: "By marrying his mother, does Oedipus exercise free will, or not?"

I asked the students to move their chairs to one side of the room or the other, depending on whether they wanted to argue for or against Oedipus having free will. But one male student refused to move his chair. He sat stubbornly by himself in the middle of the room.

Another student asked me, "How can an ancient play be relevant today?"

"Has anyone here heard of the unconscious?" I asked.

"I don't think the Greeks had the unconscious back then," a student said.

Meanwhile, the student in the middle of the room glared arrogantly at me. Hoping that he might turn out to be useful in a class on argumentation, I asked him to please defend his refusal to take a position.

"Your question has no merit," he replied.

A sharp pain invaded my lower back.

On my subway ride home, I couldn't forget the belligerent student. His attitude seemed to hold some message meant for me. I wondered: did I resemble him? Was I a fence-sitter who resentfully refused to make choices in my life? Wasn't I stubbornly trying to be both an artist and a scholar, refusing to make a choice? And regarding Charlotte, I liked being with her, but I also wanted to be completely free.

Teaching *Oedipus Rex* had touched something deep in me. It sounds like a joke, that a mother would make her ten-year-old son read that play. But back then, my mother must have been drowning in desperation over living with her severely depressed husband, whom she believed should become a king of the art world. My father, often cold to her in bed, would never fulfill his artistic potential. Maybe she had given me the play to express her inner sense of betrayal, a message to me: kill-your-father, marry-your-mother. Years later, when I was about twenty, she had guiltily confessed to me that when I was little, she had touched me sexually. I could not remember that, and I doubted that her touch had done me any harm. But the morass that was our family life at the time was another matter.

* * *

When spring came, Charlotte kept to her usual schedule, moving to Woodstock for five months. I could have taken a long bus ride to visit her, but it seemed a tedious trip. Anyway, since I had no summer teaching, I believed I should stay in the city to earn money with my art.

In July heat the sidewalks of the West Side became less crowded, while Central Park filled with people craving a breeze and some nature. Struggling trees along my street became dusty and bedraggled.

I plied my wares—small drawings and watercolors— in front of the Metropolitan Museum, and I brought two chairs to do quick portraits. We were a long row of artists and craftspeople. The grand edifice of the Metropolitan, with its billions of dollars of art treasures, has nothing in common with the street vendors outside. People looked at my work but bought nothing. I did a few portraits in pencil for seven dollars each.

I spent many hours alone in my apartment, but at the time, I didn't think that was a problem. I suppose I took some pride in being a person who could be alone; I was a loner. But my mind turned in on itself, dwelling in reflection.

At one point I took out the photo collage gift my mother had given me at our last lunch. I examined the pictures of me as a boy, arrayed around the bigger one of Eli, a grandfather whom I had never met.

My mother now seemed like a phantom I could no longer see clearly or touch in my imagination—like a TV image obscured by static. I was losing my sense of who she'd actually been. Was this my fault, or had she been, all along, a confusing, conflicted woman?

Looking at Eli, I thought of my mother's family, Jewish by blood. They had struggled financially. Eli, with a brother, had owned a dress shop that failed in the Depression. My mother's version of the story was that her father fell apart and was unwilling or unable to go out and dig ditches if necessary to earn money. His wife, my Nana, was the strong one. After the mysterious death of a first child, she became a Christian Science practitioner renowned enough to be mentioned in *Who's Who*. One of her sons, my uncle Howard, invented a spherical valve so precise that it was used on submarines. With his brother Herschel, Howard formed a company that would eventually sell for a hundred million dollars. My mother was hugely proud of Howard.

She must have wanted to be equally proud of my father, as an artist—why else would she promise me, at ten, that he would become "one of the world's ten best painters"?

But then my mother had always been ambitious, which was one reason, I suspected, why she had been entranced by my father's WASP history, with its share of famous people. There was a thick genealogy chronicling the history of the name Slocum, my father's and my middle name. Five-year-old Frances Slocum was captured by Indians in Pennsylvania in 1778, married a chief, and famously refused to rejoin white society. In Michigan in the nineteenth century, Slocums bought land rich for lumbering and mineral rights. Giles B. Slocum, in 1854, was a founder of the Republican Party; his son became a Michigan state senator. General Slocum, of the Civil War era, had a ferryboat named after him, which sank off Manhattan in 1904, drowning 1,021 passengers. My mother loved the drama, or melodrama, of it all.

But the other side of success is failure. At our last meal, she had mentioned that my face resembled her father's. Now, looking at the photo of Eli, I thought this didn't bode well for me. His eyes looked weak and gentle, not strong. Did I take after him, the man afraid to dig ditches?

Alone in my apartment, I could find no antidote for the pressure to do better. With inherited money, my artist parents had been blessed to create a kind of artists' Garden of Eden, a paradise in which they were free to create. Not selling paintings didn't seem to matter to them, whereas I must measure my talent in the larger world, with no excuse for failure. I should be proof of what was supposed to happen.

But rather than work on a painting, I lay like a castaway on my bed, remembering a dream I'd had years earlier. During high school, when I was on an all-star prep school soccer team touring England, I went to a pub with a teammate, who confessed to me that he was secretly a father. The illicit nature of his fatherhood shocked me. That night, quite drunk, I fell out of bed because of a nightmare. In it I was trying to put down clean white towels to hide my father's grotesque head, which was stuck in a toilet. Then, abruptly, the scene changed: I was outside, hanging onto the top of a speeding car driven by my mother. I reached down through the window to make her stop, but she wouldn't.

There's nothing like ambition mixed with shame to throw you out of bed in England.

6

The Best Eggs

Summer droned on.

If many people ignore their nighttime dreams, I never have. In July I dreamt that an insanely angry man was raving in the middle of Grand Central Station, brandishing a rifle at the crowd. I tried to calm him, but he wouldn't listen. So, like everyone else, I ran for an exit. As I ran, though, I heard an announcement meant only for me come over the public address system. *The best eggs are on the East Side.*

Of course I analyzed the dream. Eggs were my favorite, and most comforting, food. My only association with the East Side was that Charlotte lived there. The dream logic was clear: Charlotte had the "best eggs" in my life.

Things fell apart for me on a steamy hot Sunday. I had called up my closest city friend, Frank, whom I didn't see enough of, because he lived in Queens and worked overtime at a photography portrait studio out there. We agreed to meet in Central Park to find a pickup soccer game to play in. We joined a game near the Delacorte Theatre, where Shakespeare in the Park is put on. Originally from Sicily, Frank could play the game. Still fit in his mid-forties, he wore regular street clothes.

It was so hot and muggy that running was exhausting, but I played furiously. I had to keep up with good players from all over the world. They yelled, "Frenchy, Frenchy!" or "Spanish, hey, Spanish, pass here," or, to me, "America, over here!"

"Golasso!" High fives.

A big, suave Argentinian defenseman turned his body around and around, keeping the ball away from me. Frank had wisely quit and was resting on a nearby bench. Finally, I hobbled over to him. His broad Sicilian face still sweaty, he said, "Peter, you're not bad at this game, but why play so crazy hard?"

Frank saw a vendor and bought us orange ices.

I hadn't told him much about Charlotte. But now, for some reason, I started to talk about her. I might have been bragging, in telling Frank about her impressive apartment and how she had known famous artists and writers. Frank reacted with cynicism.

"I prefer the company of *young* people," he said. "Old people become rigid. They depress me."

"She's different," I said.

He wagged a finger in my face. "I know all about those rich Upper East Side types, who live to show off their money."

His devaluing Charlotte, sight unseen, upset me. I told myself that Frank's background, so different from mine, might explain his attitude. Emigrating from Sicily at fifteen, he had had to make it on his own. He had tossed pizzas for a living before enlisting in the Army. His family had never encouraged the life of the mind or any art, and Frank couldn't afford college. But, a true autodidact, he had read Plato and Dante as a teenager. Frank and I had met in a New School course in short-story writing. English being his second language hindered his writing. But self-reliant Frank was a believer in American opportunity, and he did not like complainers.

I asked Frank to have dinner with me on the West Side.

"Sorry, Peter, I have a wedding shoot tonight way out on Long Island." He sighed. "I tell you, my friend, I'm dying for a good vacation."

So we split up. I climbed the four floors up to my apartment and opened a bottle of gin. I'd played soccer too hard. I was making virtually nothing with my art. As I stared out the window, a strange thing happened. The angle of my apartment's floor seemed to shift weirdly. I knew it was an illusion, but my floor tilted downward, like a giant game board, funneling toward the open window, pulling me toward it with the force of gravity. Words appeared in my mind: *Throw yourself out the window.*

My fear of the open window wasn't a typical suicidal thought, either—this was in my gut, something new. It wouldn't pass, and, trying to use reason, I told myself I should call someone for help.

The Doctor? No, he was a sinking ship himself. Frank? He wasn't home, he was at a wedding shoot on Long Island. My father? No.

Low to the floor, fearful of the window, I crept toward the phone and dialed the Woodstock area code.

"Take the bus up here," Charlotte said without hesitation.

I would.

I managed to close the window, pack quickly, and take a cab to the Port Authority bus terminal.

* * *

I lay very still on Charlotte's couch, not wanting to see anyone or to be seen. Fortunately, her house was safely tucked in the woods. There was no one watching me but Charlotte, and she acted so much herself, so self-possessed, in her way, that I didn't have to worry about continually reacting to her. I could rest in safety.

I wanted to stay still and try not to think at all. It was as though I were made of fragile crystal that would break if I moved too fast or thought too hard.

Hadn't I felt somehow similar to this when I was a child? I remembered moods, sensations, when I'd hear a strange, insistent rhythm within all sounds, and at those times I'd just want to curl up. I had been an overly intense, watchful child.

My very first memory in life was of the soothingly comfy cabin room, with porthole, on our trans-Atlantic ocean liner as we returned from England. I was three. Before my memory, we'd lived in Italy and England for two years. The cabin's feeling of safe enclosure was a relief. For, according to my mother, I'd refused to eat anything the whole week before our crossing. Apparently my fear of travel had started very early. My mother said that when we arrived back in the States, I was so thin that she was afraid people would think that she was "the monster," the cause of how I looked. She meant that my father was the monster—a man impossible for children to connect with. As a toddler, she told me, I'd follow him around the room, wanting some response. Later, when he wasn't painting, he would lie for hours on a couch as though in a coma, which must have been depression.

Was I, immobilized here in Woodstock, by heredity a continuation of what my father had been?

The only people likely to come into Charlotte's house, besides quiet John the caretaker, were Jan and Ed, a local couple. A woman friend of Charlotte's had introduced her to them. They first visited her after Pat died, when she wasn't keeping up with any repairs to her house. Jan and Ed, seeing the peeling paint, old furniture, and bad plumbing, assumed that Charlotte was a decidedly poor old lady. Jan offered to clean her house for free, and Ed could get some cheap firewood—there was no heating source except fireplaces. But Charlotte insisted on taking them out for dinner. The young couple thought they should order the least expensive dishes so Charlotte wouldn't, out of pride, go into debt. But she ordered fois gras, oysters, and the like, and martinis, and paid with a credit card. Their misconception when meeting Charlotte became one of their favorite stories, because she had more money than anyone else they knew.

Ed was a jack-of-all-trades who loved buying cheap old furniture that he could repaint with bright, imaginative, patterned colors, making art. And Jan was an omnivorous reader, an outgoing Kentucky woman who cleaned houses and cooked food for Woodstock bands. She'd met Ed when he toured the South as the drummer for a band. Since Ed's parents were both deaf, he had learned signing to help his parents deal with the world. But he left his native Michigan at sixteen to, as he put it, "cut my own life."

Friendly as this couple was toward me, in my socially paranoid condition after my apartment-window fright, I couldn't make normal conversation. When Ed and Jan visited Charlotte, I said almost nothing.

But gradually, in the safety Charlotte provided, I started to notice details once more. The twin peaks of the tall spruce once struck by lightning. A white porcelain rabbit on a shelf in the living room. The slanting way Charlotte's fingers gripped the frying pan as she cooked us shad roe, which spat against the pan cover so violently that she cautioned me to stay away.

Evenings we sat on the patio. "I hear the wood thrush," she would say. She would point at three tall fir trees, the moon behind them, and say, "It looks like one of Father's Japanese prints that he collected." There was something about even the repetition of some of her stories, which formerly might have seemed tedious, that was comforting, the way a church liturgy might be.

Over a few weeks, I came back to thinking of my life as something I might be able to deal with.

For years I'd juggled the goals of trying to be an artist and an academic, or writer—pictures and words—hoping I could do both. I began to see that I was insecure because I had unrealistic ambitions. An employment counselor at the Graduate Center had suggested that I might become a prep school teacher, which had not sounded glamorous—but she had called that job "sanctuary" for a certain kind of person. I had no experience teaching high school, but I could teach English or art, and maybe coach soccer. There was plenty of time left in the summer for me to send out my résumé.

I told Charlotte of my new plan.

"Good," she said. "There are lots of schools in the city, like Dalton, where I went."

During dinner out at The Bear restaurant, I felt so hopeful, suddenly, that another idea occurred to me. I remembered Frank's remark that he was dying for a vacation. And he had a car. My father owned a house on little Swan's Island, off Mount Desert Island, far up the coast of

Maine. In my buoyant mood, I imagined the three of us going to Maine together, after I sent out my résumé. I told Charlotte my idea.

"I want to go to Maine!" she said immediately.

That was how Frank would meet Charlotte and a very odd threesome would travel to Maine.

7

Island Insight — I Love Her

A week later, my résumé mailed to seven schools, Frank and I drove up from Queens to pick up Charlotte in Woodstock. We stowed her baggage in the trunk of Frank's rusty old Lincoln Continental, so Charlotte could sleep if she wished, stretched out in the back seat. By the time we crossed Kingston-Rhinecliff Bridge over the Hudson River, she was sound asleep.

I had called my father about our trip, to make sure it was all right to use the house. If surprised that Charlotte was going, he didn't betray it. His one fatherly request of me, while in Maine, was that I please check a leaky water pump in the cellar.

Frank loved driving through the rural landscape of New England, with its small farms, dirty black and white cows, and crop fields. He was reminded of his childhood, when his grandfather had tended a large garden in Sicily.

At the border between Vermont and New Hampshire, we entered a traffic circle. Map in hand, I was supposed to tell Frank which road to take out of the circle, but I'd lost us on the map. I was flustered and embarrassed, as he kept circling around and around, waiting for me to say where to go.

Charlotte woke up. "Where's the ocean? Why are we going in circles?"

"Ah, sleeping beauty awakes," said Frank dryly. "Our navigator here can't tell me which way."

"Take a chance, for God's sake!" Charlotte said.

So I guessed. I pointed. No doubt I was wrong. Frank barreled us out of the circle.

Neither of my companions understood how fragile I could feel on trips, what one stupid mistake could do to me. In a paroxysm of self-loathing, sure that I was wrong, I began comparing myself with Frank—he was the real man on this trip, because he was doing all the driving. I seemed to shrink to the status of a little boy being driven by his father. A tiny hole in the car's rusted metal floor at my feet even reminded me of a similar hole in the back of the family's wooden-sided Plymouth when I was a child. I used to put my eye to it to watch the blur of road below.

Then Frank read a sign: "Maine. All Points North."

Relief washed over me. I was saved.

We drove on without incident to the other side of New Hampshire and pulled in at the Seacliff Inn, where I'd made us reservations. Charlotte had one room, Frank and I another. That's how it had to be, since Frank didn't know our secret.

Sitting down for dinner in the inn's dining room, Charlotte wore her Venetian gondolier's hat and a red dress with a lightning-bolt pattern. Her hat, tilted back, looked like a golden halo, showing off her "bobbed" white hair. This was the first time Frank had seen her in her full regalia.

"I feel I'm in the presence of a queen," he murmured sarcastically.

When our food was served, Frank learned more about the world of Charlotte. After a bite of her sirloin, she exclaimed, "This tastes exactly like *blotting paper*," and, using her fork, she struck her water glass so loudly that everyone in the dining room stared at us. Frank and I both cringed. Charlotte told the waiter, "This steak has been frozen! Bring me the Dover sole instead."

"Now I know how the leisure class lives," commented Frank. "I suppose my wine, even if I like it, isn't good enough, Charlotte."

"I didn't order *your* wine," shot back Charlotte. "I like good food and drink. I am not a tea-and-cookies old lady."

For the moment they seemed at a standoff.

And I worried: had I brought together two people on this trip who would do nothing but skirmish the whole time? I had an allegiance to both, being the host, so I couldn't take sides. My anxiety must have shown on my face, because Charlotte looked at me, as though reading my mind.

"Don't worry, Peter," she said. "Frank has his opinions, and so do I." And then she smiled at Frank. "Peter can be timid sometimes, other times he isn't at all. He is an enigma."

"You're right about that," said Frank. "We agree on something."

Later, in our room, our bedside lamps off, Frank smoked and I watched the red dot of his cigarette moving in the dark. He said, "Your cousin is willful. But I like her. She's very straightforward."

So I had exaggerated the problem between them. I felt so much better that my thoughts went to the other extreme. Would I, should I, dare to tell Frank the truth, that Charlotte and I were lovers? No, I wasn't up to that. I would settle for Frank seeing that Charlotte was worth knowing, was anything but ordinary. Maybe later, sometime, I could tell Frank.

***

In the morning, Charlotte insisted on paying all our inn expenses. As she asked me to, I took her American Express card to the man at the desk, so that she could sign in her room. The jovial man said, "Your mother is a real spitfire."

"She's not my mother, she's my cousin-once-removed," I said. "Much too old to be my mother."

"She doesn't look a day over seventy."

Until that moment, I hadn't quite realized the importance to me of Charlotte being seen as decidedly elderly. That way, in some hazy way I was only half aware of, I might appear to be taking care of her—instead of the other way around. I wasn't a "mamma's boy" if there was no mother.

We drove north along the coast, and in a buoyant mood, Frank began singing, "Leave the driving to us. . . . You're in good hands with. . . Franco!"

"They said that about the *Titanic*," commented Charlotte.

"I suppose you were on it," Frank joked.

"No, but my friend was."

She told us. In 1912 the whole Church family had been in France when Uncle Charlie tried to get them berths on the ship that couldn't sink. But it was all booked up. At the Folies Bergère to see dancing French girls, ten-year-old Charlotte got to drink a beer, and that's when their waiter told them of the *Titanic* disaster. It took a week before Charlotte learned that her little girlfriend and her mother had survived.

After a few more hours of driving, we were aboard the Swan's Island Ferry, standing behind a thin metal chain at the bow, above choppy, slate-gray water. Barrel-chested and stocky, Frank looked gigantic next to slender Charlotte, one hand on her Venetian hat so it wouldn't blow off. Low island shapes, like a painter's strokes of blue and green, slid slowly by, shifting in perspective, reminding me that the island was a perfect place to do watercolors.

Charlotte bet Frank that a seagull, hovering in the breeze, would swoop down to carry off someone's sandwich left on a bench. The bird did, so Frank gallantly handed over a ten-dollar bill. She happily told him about a parakeet she'd once had, and about various other pets and wild creatures that she loved—especially Bengal tigers.

I had a moment of clarity: Charlotte was herself as natural and honest as an animal. I loved her for that. The tilt of her head, the stamping of her feet when she got excited, how she sniffed the air . . . she was as true as an animal, or a child. What you saw was what you got. And I loved her.

After our ferry's hull squeaked into the wooden slip, we drove onto the island, which is shaped like a butterfly, a narrow isthmus in the middle connecting its two wings. Swan's is only five miles wide, but the island's coastline of endless inlets and spits is a hundred miles long. Only about four hundred people lived on the island. We drove past intense green fir trees and a few small white houses, some with rusted old cars and junk in the yards. We followed a mile-long dirt road ending at Stanley Point, and the house.

It was a simple two-story white box with a red-shingled roof, connected by a covered breezeway to a barn where the former owner, a fisherman, had once kept his buoys, ropes, and lobster traps. Beyond the house was Burnt Coat Harbor, a lighthouse on the opposite side, and then the open ocean.

"My God, what a view," said Frank. "What a place you have."

"It's not mine, it's my father's," I said.

I lugged Charlotte's big, scarred yellow suitcase inside and up the stairs to the master bedroom. Frank's room would be between hers and mine, back under the eaves. Right outside Charlotte's bedroom door, there was a low railing, less than three feet high, over the open stairwell. Her way to the bathroom was to turn right, away from the stairwell. I saw the danger immediately: up at night to use the bathroom, sleepy, she could plummet over the low railing. I sternly warned her.

She said I shouldn't worry, that she'd brought Halcion pills to help her sleep, probably straight through the night. In fact, would I please bring her up a bowl of soup right away so she could go to bed early? Then she whispered, "With Frank here, how are we ever going to, you know, *get together?*"

I shook my head and shrugged. Sex couldn't happen.

Going down and then back upstairs with the soup, I was reminded of my mother's aesthetic. She had refused to ruin the clean, simple look of the stairs by putting up a banister.

* * *

With Charlotte asleep, Frank took it upon himself to make us spaghetti. As we ate, he talked about his pet cat, Cady, back in Queens. Even though a friend would stop by his ground-floor apartment to feed her, Frank hated leaving Cady. He so passionately loved the cat that I kidded him, saying he was an Italian family man after all, with Cady as his child.

Swan's is a very quiet island, and we had no radio or TV to change that fact. Insisting on washing our dishes, Frank glanced out the window above the sink. "No sounds outside, no neighbors, no city sirens. Peter, I'm not used to this—it's spooky."

Driving, cooking, and now refusing to let me wash our dishes, Frank seemed intent on showing off his work ethic. Or maybe he somehow felt that Charlotte and I were more of the upper class, and he proudly working class. His attitude was getting on my nerves. But his admitting that he felt out of place, slightly spooked in Maine, gave me an idea. I told a ghost story.

"I don't want to scare you, Frank," I began, "but this house is haunted. The last owner, Austin Sprague, was a fisherman who hated off-islanders, especially the tourists he had to catch lobsters for. He died fishing in a storm at sea." I pointed at the cellar door. "In the middle of the night his ghost will come up those steps, and find you in your room."

Frank laughed and dried his hands. "Yeah, sure. Good night, Peter, I'm going up to read before I get a good night's sleep."

In the kitchen I tried to look out the big picture window, but with the bright ceiling bulb on overhead, I saw only my own face reflecting back off the glass: the fluff of my thinning brown hair, dark caves for eyes, the underbrush of my beard. Memory took me over. A dozen years ago, in bright sunlight, my mother had sat on the grass outside this same window, reading *Finnegan's Wake* aloud to herself. When I joined her, though, she stopped reading. Her face was full of anger.

"What's wrong?" I asked.

"Your father has great feeling inside him, including a capacity for sexual pleasure, but he simply *denies it all!*" Her hands balled into fists. "I won't stand for it!"

So that was why she had affairs with other men. On that particular day in Maine, she said, "I know that you, my son, can be different than your father—be strong and sensitive, both. That's a rare gift. I love you very much."

* * *

My attack of memory over, I went upstairs, but I couldn't get to sleep because I kept imagining Charlotte, hazy from her sleeping pill but going to the bathroom anyway, bumping into the low railing and pivoting over it down the stairwell.

At one o'clock I gave up and got up. I went downstairs and walked out through the breezeway and into the fisherman's shed. Beside the old hooks, lead fishing weights, and loops of rope, I found a roll of duct tape and four long strips of ceiling molding left over from renovation. Like a comedic actor in some old silent movie, I clumsily maneuvered the slender moldings into the house and up the stairs. Using the wooden stool from the bathroom to stand on, I crisscrossed the bendable moldings and taped them to the ceiling. Then I taped the bottom ends to the railing. I'd built a kind of Charlotte catcher. Brilliant, I thought. Before she could possibly fall down the stairwell, she'd bump up against the moldings. I put the stool back in the bathroom, returned to my room, and slept.

* * *

In the morning, it was all blue sky and bright sunlight. Tall grass and bushes descended down to a mosaic of rock that looked like frozen waves holding up strewn boulders and seaweed at low tide. The water was silvery pale before blending into green and then blue, and almost black with scrimshaw whitecaps far out. As I looked, Frank found me.

"Last night I saw that weird construction of yours," he said. "I thought I was in the Twilight Zone."

I started to explain, but he'd figured it out.

Frank confided that, after hearing my Austin Sprague ghost story, he'd woken, turned on his lamp, and thought he saw the ghost in his bedroom—before realizing that it was his own reflection in the window. He shrugged good-naturedly. Typical of Frank, he waxed philosophical. "We're all just scared, vulnerable human beings, I guess. Even when *we're* the ghosts."

Meanwhile, Charlotte had come out to join us.

"You won't believe this," she said. "Last night I tripped over a stool in the bathroom and fell backwards into the bathtub. It took me a half hour to get out."

I'd put the stool back in the wrong place!

Frank whispered to me that Charlotte must have only imagined it, a side effect of her sleeping pill.

But Charlotte heard him. "I *was* in the bathtub! Don't talk as though I'm not here."

Frank smirked his disbelief.

"I have all my marbles," insulted Charlotte told Frank. "I keep myself fit, mentally and physically. Watch this."

On the grass in front of us, Charlotte stood like a statue before beginning her exercise. With her back straight and arms out in the air, she slowly bent her knees to lower herself to a squat. She lay back flat for a second, did a sit-up back onto her haunches, and rose again, never touching a hand to the ground, back to a standing position.

Frank was impressed, but his expression showed that he still didn't believe her bathtub story. I fumed, angry over his disbelief. Charlotte saw the looks on our faces, our silent argument.

"For God's sakes," she said. "Doesn't anyone have a sense of humor anymore?"

Before we had coffee and breakfast out on the lawn—Charlotte in her folding aluminum chair we'd brought from Woodstock—I called my father's caretaker, Carol Loeur. She could be over in a half hour to do as I requested.

We three watched as the energetic woman in her forties, a good carpenter, sawed and hammered two-by-fours. With them, she heightened the upstairs railing and added a banister to the stairs.

Frank commented, with at least a little humor, "Some *men* would be embarrassed to watch a woman do all this work."

"On an island, you learn to do things," replied Carol.

"Men can be stupid," commented Charlotte. "I told Peter I don't need a railing—we want live *trees* more."

Carol nodded. "You know that, Charlotte, and I know that, but the men don't."

* * *

That afternoon, while Frank wandered off taking photos, Charlotte and I spent time on the fisherman's dock, she in her folding chair and I lying flat on the warm, sunlit boards. With my cap over my face, I imagined the pinprick holes in my hat were stars in a night sky.

Enjoying the sun, Charlotte decided to tell me about one of the most wonderful experiences of her life. She had been twelve when her Uncle Charlie arranged a solo overnight trip for her on a side-wheeler steamship that left New Jersey and steamed around Long Island. Feeling ecstatically independent, Charlotte saw dolphins and flying fish as the side-wheeler eventually passed within eyeshot of her own family's mansion in New Rochelle.

Listening to this, I realized something important that Charlotte and I shared. We both reveled in the contemplation of beauty, heightened by being alone. She had told me also of spending solitary hours as a child in her favorite apple tree. And, as an adult, even while married, she would wander for days by herself in her favorite city, Venice. Now I thought: we are alike in this, so maybe we can even feel the wonder while we are together.

The simple fact was that, despite our age difference, we had much in common. Our fathers were introverted artists, our mothers were socially aggressive, and both our families had independent means.

In the sunlit warmth of the dock, Charlotte reached her hand down to touch mine. We held hands for only a second, though, because Frank might wander back any time.

* * *

The following morning, a phone call ended Frank's vacation. The friend feeding his cat called, saying that Frank's apartment had been broken into and his computer stolen. The cat, terrified, would not come out from under the bed. Frank paced back and forth before deciding that he must leave the island to go home—mainly for his Cady.

So I drove him to the ferry. A short taxi ride on the mainland would take him to the Mount Desert Airport, for a small plane to start the trip back to New York. He gave me his car keys; I would later drive Charlotte back to Woodstock.

I watched Frank's bulky frame disappear into the dense fog covering the ferry slip. It had begun to rain. But I felt better: Charlotte and I were now nicely isolated by ourselves on an island, far away from the world's eyes and all the usual social context and age markers of appropriate behavior. I felt a glow of warmth for Charlotte.

But after parking back at the house, for reasons I did not understand, I was not ready to be with Charlotte. I did go into the house; she must be up in her bedroom waiting for me. My ambivalence was back. Why was I in a romance with an old lady? I realized, with some shame, that Frank's presence had lent me an "out," saving me from confronting my doubts about Charlotte.

I put on a yellow slicker from the breezeway, took a pint of Early Times bourbon from the kitchen, and started down the winding path through high bushes to the dock. Rain was falling harder, but I didn't care. I sat on the wet boards and dangled my feet over the dock's edge. My flashlight beam couldn't penetrate the fog to the water, but I could hear the seaweed sloshing and tiny stones churning below, sounding like the anxiety of my dilemma.

Was I a brave nonconformist or a freak, to be Charlotte's lover? Was I a boy hiding behind an old woman's skirts, or a man brave enough to love? I didn't know the answers.

But Charlotte was waiting for me in her room.

High on bourbon, I retraced my steps up to the house. In my flashlight beam, in the fog, the tall bushes and trees along the path looked like a fairy-tale tunnel. My foot sank into a puddle, and I stopped. In this otherworldly world, beyond reason, I suddenly remembering a story I'd loved as a kid: *Brer Rabbit*. In that story, a smart baby rabbit is caught by a fox and pleads with his captor: Please, please . . . don't throw me into the briar patch! Not there! So the fox throws him . . . exactly where Brer Rabbit really does want to be, at home in the briar patch.

So I was doing exactly what I wanted to do now.

When I got to her room, I lay down beside Charlotte on the bed. "You took so long," she said.

* * *

Over eons of time, each major inlet of the island collected its own kind of rock, from jagged, butcher-block size to smooth smaller ovals or rounder stones, from white to brilliant black. Only one inlet, Fine Sand Beach, had just that, fine sand. And with its long, flat, outward grade, only there did the water warm enough to swim in. We had the whole beach to ourselves.

Charlotte stripped down to her underpants and T-shirt to stride in up to her collar bones. "Ahhh, that feels *good*," she crooned, as I joined her in the water.

By the time we got back to the house, Charlotte was sneezing. So she asked to have a hot bath. The hot water heater was small, and so she could have a good, deep soak, I stood outside the bathroom door with extra hot water boiled on the stove to add to her tub. "Hot water!" Charlotte yelled, and I went in to carefully pour. This was not a darkened bedroom, so Charlotte shyly held up a washcloth, as though that might hide her body.

But that was beside the point, for me. Here was my problem. My role, standing at the ready with hot water, waiting for her call, made me feel too much like her servant, at her beck and call. I hid my anger at her, but I felt it.

And just then, my sense of duty reminded me of the chore my father had mentioned: to check a leaky pump. Charlotte's bath done, I went to the cellar. Down there the recent rain had created two little streams on either side of a crumbling cement floor. I looked everywhere but could not find a water pump. I found pipes and a black hose for gas to the stove above. Only one chore, and I couldn't do it.

I must have never really grown up, because again I was reminded of a childhood event, a terrifying experience at the time. When we lived in New Preston, Connecticut, not long after returning from Europe, my father gave me a simple job to perform, cleaning the TV aerial taken off the roof. Iron-faced, very serious, he handed me a rag and cleaning fluid and left me to work. But a metal prong of the aerial snapped off in my hand. Afraid of my father's vengeance, I ran away to hide in the woods across the street.

* * *

It was almost time to leave the island, using ferry reservations I had made when we came. But both I and Charlotte had lost track of exactly what day it was. Did we have one, or two, days to pack? We were lost in time.

"Call the operator and ask," said Charlotte.

I dialed. "Hello . . . I'm on an island . . . and I don't know what day it is," I said into the phone.

"August 12, sir," replied the operator.

"I meant the day of the week."

"Friday." She laughed. "I wish I was on an island and didn't know what day it was."

By our last evening, we were all packed to leave. I had not done a single watercolor that I liked, but out of nowhere, a different creative idea came to me: casting a sculpture. After balancing a round shell from Fine Sand Beach open end up in the fireplace ash, a beer can cut in half with shears was as a crucible on the red-hot coals. I melted small lead fishing weights left in the fisherman's shack, and with pliers I poured the crucible's molten metal into the shell.

Cracking open the cooled shell with a hammer, like an egg, left a cast sculpture: a shiny version of the original, once-alive sea snail. A lively looking ghost. In some way, I felt it was a symbol of my own self.

* * *

Charlotte didn't want me to feel like a chauffeur, so she rode up front with me in Frank's car. She was small in the seat, the safety belt too close to her neck, so she kept pulling it down. Fortunately, I discovered that my being solely responsible for her safety made me a more confident driver. I had the odd fantasy of being a father driving his little girl home.

I took the faster route, the Massachusetts Turnpike, instead of crossing New Hampshire and Vermont. Sniffling from the cold she'd caught, Charlotte talked a blue streak anyway, mostly about her travels in cars.

To get a license, around 1920, she had taken her driving test in a Model T. But the car stalled at a light, and the man testing her was so impatient that he got out of the car and walked away, leaving her stranded. She never did get a license. But when Bunny fell drunk in a ditch after a party, it was Charlotte who drove them home in the dark from New Rochelle to Manhattan.

She told me all about her girlhood and cars. In 1916, visiting her grandmother in Detroit, she saw how the upper-crust ladies there drove around town in their own electric cars. At tea parties society ladies served Wrigley's chewing gum, the newest thing, on silver trays. Charlotte described her own little "red bug" car, whose engine needed cranking to start, that she drove all around New Rochelle when she was little.

Good for her, I thought, but I was tired of listening. Finally I said, "Okay. I've heard enough about your perfect childhood."

"Perfect, ha!" She sat bolt upright, angry. "I'll tell you how perfect my childhood was. When I was ten, my favorite person in the world died! Elizabeth, my two-year-old sister." Charlotte turned her head, looking out her window. "Father and Uncle Charlie were away on a hunting trip when Elizabeth fell sick. She kept calling out to me, 'Sisti, Sisti!,' but Mother wouldn't let me see her, promising she'd be better by morning. In the morning Elizabeth was dead from colic. That was my perfect childhood. I'd had a *premonition*." Charlotte slumped and fell asleep.

8

Eros and Ashes

In Woodstock, before I went to the city to check replies to my teaching inquiries, Charlotte told me about her own job search, way back when. Apparently she thought her own story would encourage me.

She hadn't wanted college; she wanted to go to work. Loving books, she tried publishing first. A man at Womraths said, "So little Miss Church wants to be a proofreader? We've never hired a woman, and we never will." Charlotte applied to be a bartender, but 1920s New York wouldn't license a female bartender. Next she approached her Uncle Elihu at Church and Dwight, the family company, but he said, "Two of your cousins are interested in baking soda, and they are men."

Though disapproving of her ambition, Charlotte's father introduced her to a woman friend, Mrs. Turnbull, who ran the Walpole Gallery, an auction house, after her husband became ill. Mrs. Turnbull hired Charlotte, at twelve dollars a week. Charlotte mostly dusted art and furniture, until one day, in the crammed basement, she noticed a tiny yellow label on a Siamese chess set of inlaid mother-of-pearl and ebony. At Walpole only Charlotte could read the label's handwritten French, which she remembered, now, as reading: "Given to Louis XVI from the King of Siam, see S.S., who quotes it in his memoirs on page 50." She confirmed the truth of the quotation in the memoirs of Saint-Simon. Then Mrs. Turnbull gave Charlotte a desk next to her own, a twenty-five dollar bonus, and the chance to learn the entire auction business—a career.

Charlotte could have gone on in that career, but she decided instead to marry Bunny Schroeder, who landed his journalist job at *Time* magazine. I thought, hearing all this, that I would tell Frank about how Charlotte had proved she could work, so she never was just another rich, uptown girl.

* * *

I wanted to drive Frank's car back to him, but the nightmare maze of highways to Queens intimidated me. How pathetic. I parked by a Woodstock phone booth and called Frank to ask for his best directions, but even before I finished the question, kind Frank said, "No, Peter, take a bus—I'll get the car later."

Then he told me his news. Intent on catching the "bastard" who broke into his apartment, he left a window open. As though no one were home, he waited in the dark with a baseball bat.

"At three in the morning, Peter, a head appeared in the window, but I couldn't smack him! I don't know why."

"Thank God, Frank. You're not a Mafioso, after all."

"Here's the unbelievable part. I ran out into the street after the bastard and halfway down the block before I realized I was only in my underwear."

"Nice work."

"He got away. But here's my point, Peter. After being out there in my shorts, now I do believe Charlotte's story in Maine, because that's how strange life is. She really *was* in that bathtub."

* * *

Only one school, an all-girls prep school in northwestern Connecticut, asked me for an interview. By chance the school was an hour's drive from Kent, so I took a train north to borrow a car from my father. I owed him a visit anyway.

Picking me up at Dover Plains, even inside his blue Ford Tempo, my father wore a wide-brimmed straw hat and sunglasses to protect his skin from sunlight. As a teenager, severe psoriasis had almost killed him, and it made his skin prone to cancers. When I was a child, he had constantly scratched his fingertips across his face, arms, and ears, making a weird whipping sound. His skin had calmed down since then, but an operation on a cancerous eyelid kept it from closing completely.

As we drove he asked if I felt ready for my interview. What could he possibly know about job hunting?

"I hope you don't mind helping me with something in town," he said. "I'm mailing your mother's ashes." He had finally finished designing the headstone. As agreed, half the cremains were to be buried in the family plot that my Uncle Howard had created on Cape Cod.

My father described the double headstone for my mother and himself. He'd settled on a quote carved in the stone, from one of her favorite Chinese poems by Tzŭ Yeh: "Do you not see that you and I are as the branches of one tree?"

One tree? He seemed to claim a warmth between them that had never existed.

The House of Books, where my father had had his show and I had had my book signing, did UPS mailing. We parked, and he took a cardboard Dewars box containing the urn of ashes out of the car. We went inside. The woman at the counter directed us to a back room, where we could prepare the package. She treated my father with great respect, even though, to me, he resembled a cheap imitation of Truman Capote in his oversized straw hat and dark glasses.

My father suggested we work together, he pulling brown paper from a roller for me to cut; he folding the paper around the box for me to tape down. Working efficiently like this with him had almost never happened before.

It was a good moment for me to confess: I told him that I had never located the leaky water pump in Maine, and apologized for not calling him.

"Not your fault!" He smiled, oddly amused. "Carol called the other day to tell me it's a *submerged pump*, thirty feet down in our well! I thought it was in the cellar."

My father's good humor about his own ignorance surprised me. Some fathers and sons might be bonded by being "handy," but we were alike in not being so. And maybe, it occurred to me, my father had mellowed a bit since my mother's death.

After the desk lady took the wrapped package, while my father went to buy a newspaper, I lingered, looking at books. The lady approached me. "Peter, I was so sad when I heard about your mother. I must tell you how I've admired your parents over the years. They were the only couple I ever knew who could eat lunch in the same restaurant at the same time *at different tables.* They cared not a whit what other people thought. So independent-minded! You've been very lucky."

Was I? I had never looked at it that way.

I walked with my father to Kent's Fife and Drum Restaurant. For dinner, he had swordfish, and I had the duck. He drank scotch, and I drank a dry martini, Charlotte style.

"So how did Charlotte like the island?" he asked.

She'd loved the house, the views, birds, deer, and even swimming in the cold water, I said.

Betraying a grimace, he said, "Yeah, it wouldn't surprise me if she *walked on the water.*"

Then, embarrassed by his tone, he tried to explain. "You know, growing up in the Midwest, I used to envy Charlotte's sophistication. Her living in Manhattan, traveling the world, knowing famous people, all that. But later, when I really got to know her, we read poetry together, and I grew fond of her." He paused for another sip of his scotch. "I love her, really. Unfortunately, over the years, we got out of touch."

Now I knew how left out he must have felt when Charlotte went to his Maine house with me.

* * *

At the Kent house, after my father went to bed, I stayed up trying not to obsess about my interview in the morning. I told myself that, in all likelihood, I wouldn't like the school or the job, anyway. Then, thinking about our mailing the ashes reminded me that the other half of my mother's cremains must still be in my father's studio. The two martinis I'd had at dinner no doubt encouraged what I did next.

I took a kitchen cup and a flashlight, and went out to my father's separate studio building. It was a large working space I envied: two stories high, buttressed by huge barn beams, a bank of north windows for painting light. I found the plastic box of ashes on my father's shelves for poetry first editions, between Ezra Pound and Wallace Stevens. With my teacup, I scooped out a bit of the cremains.

I went outside and walked to the giant cement silo that still stood, by itself, some thirty feet away from a small remaining part of what had once been a big dairy barn. The original three-story barn, with its trap doors and myriad hiding places, had been my favorite place to play as a kid. I switched on my flashlight, pulled myself up to the silo's opening, and dropped down inside.

My feet echoed on the concrete floor as barn swallows twittered. I balanced the flashlight at the center of the floor so the beam shined upward, as the swallows, chased by their shadows, whirled upward in circles to escape through an opening at the top.

I was here to perform a private ceremony with my mother's ashes. But how, I was not sure. Holding the cup of ashes, I sat down with my back against curved cement, and closed my eyes. For a long time now my mother had seemed too much like a ghost to me. How could I feel closer to her, make her—even if only in memory—more real?

I poured the cremains onto my palms, and rubbed my hands together. Powdered bone. At least I was showing her that I wanted to understand her better. Could it be that the suddenness, the unexpectedness of her death had angered me, so that I was somehow cheating myself out of a clearer picture of her?

For a long moment I seemed lost in time. I thought of the succession of women I had known in my life—that other species of the human race, females. Perhaps for no other reason than wanting relief, I felt a sexual urge. But no, that was only part of it. Inevitably, the woman I was thinking of was Charlotte—clear, direct, knowable.

* * *

In the morning, I drove to the school. I saw right away that this girls' school in Washington, Connecticut, had a friendlier ambience than most boys' schools, such as the one I had attended, with its imposing, prideful columns and bricks. This school had mostly wooden buildings, more like houses. Greeting me, the headmaster, about forty, was dressed in a simple shirt and jeans, and he took me immediately to the art building. Inside was a light-filled studio space with long tables.

"We're big on interdisciplinary approaches," he told me. He said he liked my flexibility, that I might teach studio art and art history and an English course, and perhaps coach soccer. I and a woman with more teaching experience were in the running for the job. We talked about graduate school, since the headmaster himself was still completing his English PhD. And he mentioned that prep school life could become overly insular, by way of saying that I would be free to live off-campus.

He seemed to like me. A committee would decide that very evening whom to hire. The headmaster would call me in the morning.

I left excited, wanting the job. My cynicism and doubts completely dropped away, and I imagined a whole new life. This could be my solution.

Back at the house, to my amazement, my father suggested that, if I got the job, I might live in his studio and commute to work. The space had its own kitchen and bath. "Pay some rent, if that feels right, if you want," he said. "Who knows, we might get along."

"I'll . . . consider that," I said, not quite ready to let him see how good the idea made me feel. Was it possible that all this time, it had been my own unsettled life that had made me resent my father? To live a normal life, to have work I liked, and to know my father—all this seemed suddenly a possibility.

In the morning the headmaster called. The committee had chosen the other teacher. I said little to my father, just borrowed a car to drive to Woodstock.

9

My Proposal

A rare, fragile insect, a "walking stick," moved its twiglike legs slowly across Charlotte's sunlit, glass-topped patio table, its pale reflection moving with it. But I was in no mood to appreciate nature.

"Get yourself a drink, and tell me what happened," said Charlotte.

"I didn't get the job."

"Stick to your guns. You'll get something next time. *Sláinte.* That's 'to your health' in Gaelic."

I almost hated her for her good cheer. Why had I stupidly let myself be so optimistic?

Charlotte grabbed my hand. "Come, let's go for a walk."

I didn't budge at first, but her age—my hesitation to pull away forcibly—gave her an ironic power. She led me by the hand off the patio and around the corner of her house. "Look at the snowball bush," she commanded, and I saw its petal clusters like softballs touched with pink. As we continued walking, she pointed at the row of ragged little trees along her driveway. "Dogwoods, they'd do better with more light." At the end of her driveway, she finally let go of my hand so nosy neighbors wouldn't see, and we walked up Hillman.

I couldn't stop feeling like a fool for wanting a job that I couldn't get, and now my failure seemed worse because I'd run to an old woman for sympathy. Enraged, with no place to put it, I squatted and ground my fist into the road. Summing it all up, I said, "I'm a basket case."

Charlotte bristled. "No! I saw real basket cases in the Red Cross—soldiers without arms and legs."

I followed her to the end of Hillman Road, where she stepped onto a tiny wooden footbridge over a streambed that, in late summer, was only dry leaves and stones. I stepped onto the bridge.

"You have an artist's imagination," Charlotte said. "That can make things harder. Pat had that, too. Don't give up. Look, I see a trickle in the leaves."

It was a tin can reflecting light, which she mistook for water. But Charlotte's words made my shoulders heave, broke my anger, let my eyes fill with tears. Steadying my breath, I apologized. "I'm sorry, I'm just disappointed."

* * *

Before nightfall, Jan and Ed called to invite Charlotte to a party, and me also, since I was there. I couldn't refuse to drive us to it.

Jan and Ed's house was owned by a successful gay couple, interior decorators, for whom they did caretaking. We walked past a long line of parked cars, toward palpably blaring party music. Inside, people were dancing. Charlotte exclaimed in my ear, "Those girls are tall as *giraffes!*"

Jan brought us martinis, and Ed leaned down to give Charlotte a kiss on the cheek.

"What an odd chandelier," Charlotte said to him. Speaking loudly to be heard above the music, Ed explained that it was no chandelier, but a revolving video camera that he had set up to show 360 degrees of the party on a big screen by the wall. Proud of his inventiveness, he took me aside and said, "Man, I hear you draw like a maniac. I don't draw, but I've got a million art ideas. Maybe we could collaborate sometime."

Then he asked Charlotte to dance, and I watched as he showed her off as a kind of celebrity—decades older than anyone else, stylish in her black beret and Mondrian dress, and performing a 1920s step. Meanwhile, I got myself another drink, and with it I wandered out the door and looked at trees. Then I was back inside for another drink, feeling good. I asked a sexy giraffe in a miniskirt to dance, and we did, and I felt I was at the coolest party I'd been to in a long time.

I'd worked up a sweat, and with another drink, I looked around for Charlotte. I found her sitting alone on a bottom step of the front stairway. Feeling wobbly, I sat down beside her.

Charlotte sadly said, "I waited for you to dance. But now I'm all tired out."

It wasn't as though I'd ignored her on purpose. Why shouldn't I enjoy myself at a party of people my own age? But looking at her, I felt a rush of something like pride: Charlotte had more authentic style and class, even more beauty, than any of the young giraffes. An overwhelming affection for her came over me, so I leaned close. "I love you," I said. And kissed her on the mouth.

"Not in front of everyone!" she said. "You must be drunk."

The last thing I would remember was Ed on one side of me and Charlotte on the other, walking me out the door.

* * *

I woke sometime the next morning in the library room of Charlotte's house. How had we gotten home last night? I crept quietly, unsteadily, past her, still sleeping in her room. When I looked out the front door, my car wasn't there. But sitting on the bench was a video camera with a note that read, "Peter, here's my back-up video camera—experiment and enjoy! Ed."

I'd never used a video camera before. Hangover or not, I put my eye to the viewer and, with the zoom lens, learned that I could seem to fly through the air, moving from a close-up of a ladybug to far-away trees. I could capture images that would take years to paint. I liked to tell stories with so-called "narrative" pictures, and in this camera was a new world of possibilities.

I went inside, where Charlotte was up and making pancakes. I recorded her hands pouring Bisquick from a yellow box into a blue bowl; then I panned down to her red shirt, blue jeans, sneakers, and back up to the concentration of her brow. The camera would record even the sound of Bisquick sputtering in the skillet.

"I don't want to be on television," said Charlotte, putting one hand up. Her voice was serious. "Do you remember anything? You were so *tight* that Ed and I had to walk you to his truck. You said we were the Three Musketeers. They'll bring your car later."

As we ate pancakes, she sat stiff in her chair and demanded again to know how much I remembered. "In vino veritas," she said. "Do you remember what you told me?"

"Sure."

She stared at me. "Well, did you mean it?"

"Yes. I said I love you."

"Good." Her back slumped with relief. "Now pour yourself more syrup."

My memory of what I'd said was intact, but her question bothered me. What did she expect, that if I loved her, I should never enjoy myself with any younger women?

"You know, I have to feel free," I said softly. It was the idea of freedom more than about younger women.

It took her a moment to consider this. "All right, then. You can see all the young ladies you want, and still come back to the old lady."

In my mind, at least, we'd forged a deal.

* * *

The idea of marriage came to me that same day. My mind was floating more freely than usual, and maybe I was still a bit high from the booze and the thrill of the video camera. The image of Charlotte making pancakes, in particular, her care in preparing food, stayed with me.

A few hours after our midday breakfast, Charlotte sat in the living room reading a *New Yorker*. I went in and sat beside her. Pale, clear light came in through the high artist's windows, and I imagined us giving a grand party in this house. Our guests would be a wonderfully varied crowd—from young people like Ed and Jan to older, talented luminaries of the Woodstock art and music community. We'd serve champagne and caviar. My paintings would be on the walls instead of Pat's. Now a real host also, a partner with Charlotte, I would be relaxed and confident. Our uniqueness as a couple would shine.

"I have an idea," I said.

"What? Spit it out."

"For you and me, something unusual."

"Let's go to Venice," she said.

"I mean something else."

"Don't beat around the bush."

"We could get married."

"Why not?" she said, so fast that I almost felt robbed of it being my idea. She squeezed my hand. "But I think we should go to Venice first."

And that's how we decided to go to her favorite city—it would be a kind of honeymoon before marriage. There was just enough time left in August to make travel plans and go, before I returned to teaching in the city.

In the front of the house, there was a tiny guest room off the living room, and we got up and went in and made love there. Even if it hurt, Charlotte said, she wanted to do it the regular way. I'd never penetrated her before, so I was wary, but she insisted. I went very slowly and carefully.

She would tell me later that she had her first orgasm with a man that day. Though she'd enjoyed sex with Pat, it wasn't until middle age that she reached orgasm at all, and that was only by herself. Some woman friend had enlightened her, encouraged her to touch herself. Listening to this, I wondered how many women earlier in the century might never have gotten there, even been labeled "frigid," simply because of some standard of proper behavior. Charlotte had needed the right situation. It might seem an odd metaphor for sex, but I thought of her as being like a great long distance runner—if she'd been shy, or just more interested in other things in her youth and middle age, she'd woken up and was now making great strides sexually, at an age when most other women were quitting.

10

Venice Mysteries

We took off from Kennedy Airport on Alitalia, business class. Before the plane rose, Charlotte delighted in her "free" slippers, pointing her toes and saying, "My feet feel warm and free."

As the plane took off, though, she fell silent. Her eyes looked large as saucers, frightened, and she confessed that she was deathly afraid of flying. She'd always, since 1906, crossed the Atlantic only by ship, and she'd done that more than thirty times. As we leveled off at thirty thousand feet, a saving grace arrived in the form of her Alitalia manicotti, good food that distracted Charlotte enough to help her relax. Then, of course, she started to talk, telling me all about her many ship crossings of the Atlantic, her adventures.

For her a transatlantic ship had been like a second home. As an adult, aboard the British *Empress of Scotland*, in the Palm Room, she recognized chairs she'd sat in thirty years earlier, as a child. This was because the ship had once been German, the *Kaiserin Auguste Victoria*, taken by the British as World War I reparations.

In 1924 Charlotte honeymooned aboard ship with Bunny. Two of Bunny's former schoolmates at St. Mark's prep school happened to be on board, but they inexplicably snubbed Charlotte. Only in the bar did one of their girlfriends spill the beans, telling Charlotte that at St. Marks, brilliant Bunny, who won poetry prizes, had also been known as a "faggot." That was how Charlotte learned—on her honeymoon—that her husband had tastes that would, eventually, help end their marriage.

Aboard ship, after divorcing Bunny and before meeting Pat, Charlotte met Ghilberto and Aldo, Italian friends traveling together. "Ghilberto was the handsomest man I ever met, including Pat," Charlotte told me now. "Ha! When Ghilberto said, 'I feel hot' on the ship, I thought he meant the *weather*. So I invited him to my stateroom for a cold drink, and he instantly took off all his clothes." She declined his offer, because she preferred his average-looking friend Aldo. Son of a Florentine jeweler, Aldo would rave "Plastico! Plastico!" about the new plastics industry, which he hoped to get into. Later, Charlotte became pregnant by Aldo, but though he pleaded with her to have his child, she would not. She didn't love him enough for that, so she had an abortion. She was about to meet Pat Collins, whom she truly loved.

With Pat Charlotte made many Atlantic crossings, to and from Venice. It wasn't all roses, though. Pat painted so obsessively in their stateroom that it could drive Charlotte crazy. On one crossing she ate so much caviar that she got boils, and she sought out the ship's doctor for relief.

Charlotte napped while I watched the airplane movie. But before we descended to Milan, she woke and told me, "I am descended from a doge, a sixteenth-century ruler of Venice." That was hard to believe, but she claimed she'd researched it.

* * *

After taking a train from Milan, we walked out of the Venice station to stone steps leading directly down into water. It was raining, so a gondolier offered us a large white umbrella for our dripping, misty, ethereal gondola ride to the Europa Hotel, where Charlotte had booked us small, lavish, connecting rooms.

Before doing anything else, Charlotte insisted we go right away to famous Harry's Bar. On the way, we stopped by a canal where she and Pat had once encountered Katherine Hepburn acting for the movie *Summertime*. "She recognized Pat and ran into his arms," said Charlotte, "because they knew each other from doing summer stock in Woodstock." I remembered that Pat was an actor, too, and had an appetite for the limelight.

Harry's Bar was so crowded that the maître'd told us we must wait to be seated. But Charlotte told him in no uncertain terms, "I'm a friend of Harry's! I was here when he invented your peach bellini. Tell his son Charlotte Collins is here."

The maître'd returned with a small folding table and put it down for us, so we were instantly served. I conceded to Charlotte, "Maybe you *are* descended from a doge."

She smiled cunningly, and said, "And you are my *cicisbeo*."

She wouldn't explain what that meant, only that I could look it up in a book we'd brought, Maurice Rowdon's *The Silver Age of Venice*.

I'd first thought of this as a kind of honeymoon trip, but I wasn't keeping that idea in mind, because I was feeling weirdly spacey and on edge.

After we got back to our hotel rooms, before bed Charlotte slipped into a new robe she'd bought for the trip. The bathrobe was all swirls of pink and blue pastel, which unfortunately tended to bring out any bluish veins or pink spots of her skin. She looked best in her usual strong, primary colors. But feeling odd and nervous, I wasn't up to telling her she had made a bad choice of robe, the look of which made me feel almost queasy.

Charlotte was finally tired, so without any flirtations, we said goodnight. Before I went into the adjoining room, she mentioned that, since she would sleep very late in the morning, I should "go out and do whatever your little heart desires."

Her words "little heart" bugged me. Was I a "little person"? In my room, I opened *The Silver Age of Venice* to find out what Charlotte had meant at Harry's Bar by calling me her . . . *sissy-something*. As I looked for the word, I read a bit about how the famous Carnevale in Venice had been a time when normal laws of society were suspended, when disguises helped all levels of citizens meet and mix.

I found that the word started with a *c*, not an *s*. I read that in sixteenth-century Venice, a *cisisbeo* was a well-to-do woman's "companion," selected after marriage and agreed upon by the husband. The *cisisbeo* attended events and parties with the wife, as "a kind of foppish necessity; no fashionable husband can lift up his head while his wife lacks her 'servant.'"

So she had called me her servant! Sometimes with her I felt like one, but to be told it to my face was too much.

I did not sleep well.

And in the morning, I still had that peculiar, spacey feeling. In my suitcase I had a vial of Xanax, which the Doctor had given me. It was actually his own prescription. He'd said that it would help me relax. But the vial was empty now; I'd finished them all.

I went first to Saint Mark's Square, filled with squadrons of tourists plowing through clouds of pigeons rising and falling. My own mood seemed to rise and fall like the birds, in a disturbing rhythm. Off the square, I saw, behind the church, the famous Bridge of Sighs, over which Casanova had been led to prison. With my art materials from my pack, I tried a quick watercolor of the bridge, but my proportions were wrong. I couldn't believe that I was having such a hard time having a good time in Venice.

I boarded a vaporetto up the Grand Canal, planning to get off at Rialto Bridge. But it was so packed with people during their Venice morning rush hour, jostling and saying *"s'cusa, s'cusa,"* that before I knew it, we were in the shadow of the Rialto. By the time I exited, at the next stop, I saw a maze of small streets. Going down one, wandering, I was lost in Venice.

I came across a padlocked gate with a plaque that said "Ghetto Judaeca," the Jewish ghetto. So wasn't I the wandering Jew, son of a Jewish mother.

I sat down by the gate. When my family lived in Athens, Greece, for my eighth-grade year, we had visited Venice, but we never bothered to see this ghetto where Jews were forced to live. For unknown reasons, my mother had been reticent about acknowledging that she was Jewish. As a teenager, at our kitchen table, I had once asked her about her Jewish background. Without a word, she picked up her empty coffee cup and threw it at my head. My father said she wasn't being fair, so she threw his cup at me as well. She missed, but I never asked again.

Now a story Charlotte had told me came to mind. She and Bunny had traveled by train through Germany in the '30s, and stopped for lunch in a town. Their young waitress had seemed so nervous that later Charlotte thought she must have been terrified of being taken away by the Nazis.

I stood up. My only problem at the moment was being lost in Venice. I kept walking and, by luck, soon found my way back to Saint Mark's Square, where I saw Charlotte happily having a coffee at an outdoor café.

It was later, that evening, as we walked back from dinner, that I finally said to Charlotte, "You shouldn't have called me a *cisisbeo*."

She smiled. "It was a joke. Don't take life serious, it's too mysterious."

A bit drunk, and still disoriented, as I'd been all day, I went and took a pee against a wall in the shadows. When I returned to her, she took my hand and said, "At night all cats are gray."

What in hell did that mean? I felt like I was in some kind of Venetian Carnevale that I did not understand. Was her remark about disguises? Or about sex? Did she mean that all women— all cats, of any age—were alike in the dark, old or not?

Back at the hotel, Charlotte led me into the Europa's lounge, where she asked the piano man to play her favorite Italian song, *Quando Quando*, so we could dance. While dancing, suddenly I realized one reason I'd been anxious all day: before this trip I'd taken too many Xanax, too quickly, and then suddenly stopped completely. I was having withdrawal symptoms. That was it. Damn the Doctor for giving me the stuff in the first place. But having an answer calmed me.

In our rooms I finally felt more comfortable. I was able to politely tell Charlotte that her new robe was not a good choice. She thanked me—she wouldn't wear it. We made love.

Now I was ready to enjoy the Accademia, the Peggy Guggenheim, the churches, the Giudecca, all of Venice.

* * *

After regaining comfort with Charlotte that night, I wondered how many more times in my life, as in Venice, I would turn a corner and become lost. But for the moment, I could sleep with Charlotte's face in my mind. She wore no mask. I could trust her luminous face, and I was lucky to exist in its light.

11

Groom 39, Bride 86

In Manhattan we took a cab south on Henry Hudson Parkway toward City Hall, to get our marriage license. When traffic backed up to a standstill, our cabbie shrugged, "Construction." Charlotte was easily frustrated by traffic, partly because she remembered what seemed a better time in the city: the '20s, when her own 68th Street had been two-way, and when she could run a tab with her favorite cabbie and pay him at the end of the week. New York had been a smaller town.

But in the present, we were stalled in traffic.

Charlotte opened her window and lit up a cigarette. Though a rational person, she had a weird superstition that by smoking, she could change traffic flow. She had the same magical thinking about buses. Waiting for the bus with me to go to the opera, she would light up and say, "This will do it, you watch, the bus will come now." I told her that it was only the distraction of smoking that made time seem to pass faster. She would have none of it. She was irrational about the weather, as well, but with that, time sped up. If she saw on TV that a hurricane was brewing near Florida, she thought the same storm could reach us in two hours.

Her cigarette finished, she tossed it out the taxi window. Traffic moved, we moved. "See, it worked," said Charlotte.

At Brooklyn Bridge our cab entered lower Manhattan, and we got out at 100 Centre Street. Inside, after taking the elevator and walking down an empty hallway, I opened a nondescript brown door marked

City Clerk. Here was a packed mass of humanity, noises and smells, replete with numbers of children.

Charlotte nudged me, "Don't any of these people use birth control?"

"Shsh," I whispered.

"Don't be so self-conscious. Nobody's listening."

I found Charlotte a bench seat before joining the "Get Certificates Here" line, and brought back a form with the headings "From the GROOM" and "From the BRIDE." I hadn't anticipated what information was required. Since my great aunt had married Charlotte's father, my own name, Nichols, was also Charlotte's mother's maiden name, required on the form. And I had to enter our ages: 86 and 39.

Getting into the "Certificates Typed Here" line, I imagined the lady behind the Plexiglas staring at me in judgment, shocked at our information. But she didn't even look up, just typed and pushed the finished form back.

Charlotte, meanwhile, had made friends with a tiny black boy on the floor in front of her bench. "Patty-cake, patty-cake," Charlotte sang as she and the boy patted hands.

"Hi, hi!" he yelped back to her.

The boy's mother, a huge, big-busted, smiling woman, said to Charlotte, "What a beautiful dress that you're wearing, with the butterflies on it. We have many butterflies in Jamaica."

"Don't tell me about butterflies," replied Charlotte. "When I was a girl, I caught them with my bare fingers, like this." She held up her thumb and index finger. "In 1921 in your Jamaica, my father discovered a new species of butterfly."

"In the rainforest?" asked the mother.

"No, in a parking lot!"

They both laughed.

"It's been so nice to meet you," said the mother.

In the elevator Charlotte told me that the mother had reminded her of a Jamaican maid she once had. "Eloise was also round and roly-poly, and very nice, but driven crazy from worrying about her illegitimate son.

Only I knew her secret, so one day I told Eloise to take the day off—relax, go to the movies!"

Was that the end of the story? No.

"I knew the theater Eloise went to. Ha! It had a moon and stars painted on the ceiling for decoration. Do you know what crazy Eloise asked me when she came back?"

I was too distracted to care.

"'What do they do at that theater *when it rains?*'"

I couldn't laugh: we had sixty days to decide if we would marry, before the license expired. Did we dare do it?

12

A Cooking Lesson

"I'm not doing all the cooking if we marry," Charlotte told me. She had cooked for two very particular husbands, and she wouldn't do that again. I would need to learn some things. She got out *The Joy of Cooking*, and asked me to read aloud the recipe for calf's brains au beurre noir.

I gave her a mock salute, a soldier of the kitchen.

"Cooking is chemistry," she said. From her ancient Hotpoint refrigerator, she took out a bowl in which she already had two brains floating in water with lemon juice. She carried a brain to the sink, and under warm, flowing tap water, she demonstrated how to use a sharp knife to tease off the outer membranes. She said that removing the inner membranes without the brain falling apart required careful use of one's fingers. "Ach! My fingertips aren't sensitive enough anymore. You take over." She handed me the brain.

I held it up like a skull in *Hamlet*. "Dear Yorick."

"This is not a joke," Charlotte said. "This is serious."

The delicate, tactile work with the brain was kind of fun, actually. After I finished both brains, we put them back in the fridge for a half hour, to keep them firm.

Meanwhile, Charlotte quizzed me. "What does 'au beurre noir' mean?"

"Burnt in the night?"

"Browned butter! Concentrate!"

For the asparagus, Charlotte must search her string drawer for string, which we tied around the stalks in groups, so they could balance in the boiling water, tips up. The patience required for all this was beyond me.

Browning the brains in a skillet, fortunately, was quick and easy, and soon we were sitting in the dining room, ready to eat. I had dined on brains before, and this was as good as at a restaurant.

Charlotte told me that she had often prepared luncheons in the '30s for Bunny and his Time, Inc., colleagues, after they had "put the magazine to bed." Preparing a soufflé for them, she once accidentally dropped a spatula behind the Hotpoint refrigerator. In retrieving it, she discovered wads of unpaid bills that Bunny had stuck back there, including many from the psychiatrist that Bunny had promised he was seeing regularly.

I did not interrupt to ask why he needed psychotherapy, or why he had childishly hidden unpaid bills.

Charlotte visited the psychiatrist to get to the bottom of whatever was going on with Bunny. She wore her hat with a long feather sticking out its front. In his office the psychiatrist told her that Bunny, after one session, had never returned for more of his scheduled appointments. But since he hadn't canceled them, all must be paid for.

Charlotte reluctantly wrote him a check.

Then the psychiatrist suggested that Charlotte should see him herself, about her own problems. Charlotte pointed her hat's feather at his eyes and said, "I have no problem, because I am divorcing Bunny."

"You never will, because you have a mother complex."

"You just watch me!"

Shortly after that, Charlotte went to Reno and got the divorce. While in Reno, she took a course in mining and precious metals, met interesting people, and generally had a good time.

As I finished my asparagus, Charlotte delivered the moral of her story, which I hoped would never apply to me. "The worst thing about Bunny wasn't his drinking, or even that he liked men," she said. "It was his lying."

13

The Money Angle

Charlotte controlled most of her money, but she also received income from trusts. Wanting me to become familiar with "the money angle," as she called it, she invited me to a trust meeting.

The Morgan trust offices were at 6 West 57th Street. The façade of the building was a giant concave curve of white stone forty-something stories high. As I waited there to meet Charlotte and her lawyer, I watched an elderly black man slowly push two shopping carts lashed together along the gutter, maneuvering around a parked stretch limo. New York is like that: so many stark images of the haves and have-nots side by side. Manhattan can often be surreal. I'd once watched a completely naked man galloping on horseback north against traffic up Sixth Avenue. He might have been hired by some ad campaign, or done it on a bet. Like other New Yorkers, I took it in stride and didn't expect an explanation.

A yellow cab pulled up, and Charlotte and her lawyer got out. Eric M. had once been my father's lawyer, as well. I knew how much Charlotte liked him and his wife, Nancy, because she took them to the opera every year. About sixty, with sandy-colored hair, Eric looked up at the white curve of the Morgan building, and, smiling, said to me, "I read that the curve makes people nervous because it looks like it can't support itself."

We went into the building.

A Mrs. Fitz, in a gray suit, showed us into a conference room decorated with old-fashioned vine-and-flower wallpaper, English foxhunting prints, and a fireplace with birch logs.

I'd once been to a financial meeting with my father, but he obviously didn't have Charlotte's clout. The aura of the room weirdly reminded me of the Museum of Natural History, with its hermetic arrangements of stuffed animals in their natural habitats—except that here the label would read, "North American WASPs with Money."

"This is called the New England Room," said Mrs. Fitz.

"I'm not a Yankee, I'm New York," said Charlotte.

Mrs. Fitz, new to the position of managing Charlotte's trusts, might have underestimated her client. We sat down at a round table, and a black waitress handed out menus. Appetizer choices were lobster bisque or crab cakes.

Charlotte, in a rueful voice, remarked that Morgan's empty hallways meant that business couldn't be good. In a restrained voice, Mrs. Fitz insisted that business *was* good. Charlotte countered that shops all over the city were deserted. Mrs. Fitz kept a tight smile on her face. After more pleasantries were exchanged, we ate our appetizers. Up next, filet mignon or poached salmon.

There was no rush at all. The pace seemed to silently shout: there is no need to talk about money yet because the client has plenty of it.

Charlotte told a story about J. P. Morgan's nose. A young waitress, warned not to think too much about the great financier's huge nose, had offered him cream for his coffee by saying, "Nose in your coffee?"

Finally Mrs. Fitz said that all four of Charlotte's trusts—created by her mother, father, uncle, and aunt—were doing "just fine," but she spoke in a patronizing tone, as though Charlotte were an old lady with no wits.

"Father could have *wallpapered* this room with his worthless stock certificates during the Depression," Charlotte said. "Mother's bonds got us through. I want more *bonds*."

"We shouldn't incur undue capital gains by selling your Church and Dwight too quickly," said Fitz.

"Taxes!" Charlotte yelled. "I remember when there *wasn't any income tax!* Uncle Charlie said it would be the end of everything."

Fitz seemed speechless.

In the silence, completely off the subject, Charlotte remarked, "My cousin Peter here is a very good *artist.*" She must have been making a point about values, what was important in life, but I squirmed.

"Bonds," said Charlotte, her mind back to business.

On cue, Eric stepped in. He told Fitz to please draw up a selection of bonds for Charlotte to choose from.

Then came a surprise, especially for me. Mrs. Fitz passed out a chart she had worked up of Charlotte's family tree. She said that for one trust, created by her mother, Charlotte had the power to will its capital to anyone in her extended family.

Glancing at the chart, I saw my own name at the bottom. A horizontal line went from Charlotte's mother to her brother Pecks, my grandfather, and so down my side of the family.

I felt like Alice in Wonderland after tasting a magic cookie: suddenly I was bigger, more important, and belonged at this table—a potential heir. I was fully, excitedly, engaged, because several million dollars could be willed to me.

But then Eric interceded.

With a sympathetic glance my way, he told Mrs. Fitz that she had misread the trust. Its capital could *not* be willed "laterally" to my side of the family. I shrank back to normal size.

The meeting was over. Handshakes all around.

Outside on the sidewalk, Eric had one more point of business. He told Charlotte that she could call him anytime before nine at night about changing her will as she had mentioned. Apparently, though she had not told me, Charlotte wanted to change it right away, *before* the last day our marriage license was good for.

We said goodbye to Eric.

For a relaxing change-of-pace from finances, we walked up Fifth Avenue toward the Central Park Zoo, where Charlotte was a longstanding member. Yes, she replied as we walked, she knew that our marriage license was good for only three more days.

First we saw the penguins, which looked to us too much like sad bachelors in black tuxedos standing on their whitewashed cement. So we went to the polar bears. We watched a giant polar bear plunge underwater, turn a somersault, and undulate toward our underwater window. He stared straight at us with big black eyes. "The male of the species," commented Charlotte.

Outside, we sat on a bench. Charlotte said that when she and Pat had gone out to fancy restaurants, Pat had had a terrible habit of constantly looking around for celebrities he knew or wanted to meet, and in this way he'd ignored her.

"That's what I like about you," she said. "You're like the polar bear. You look me right in the eye."

14

A Dinner and a Vow

In case we did get married, Charlotte had asked Wynne, a friend since childhood, to be a witness when we went to a justice of the peace. Wynne happily agreed. I'd met Wynne a number of times, and we liked each other. Wynne was liberal-minded, like Charlotte, but had a restrained, formal manner that contrasted with Charlotte's impulsiveness. When they had dinner at nearby Shabu-Shabu restaurant, Wynne always ordered only the maguro, and each time Charlotte tried to convince her to try other varieties of raw fish. But Wynne had been adventurous in her life. She had been a serious sculptor, creating many stone and bronze mermaids. When young, she and Alberto Giacometti were the only private students of a famous sculptor. Wynne had told me she'd disliked Giacometti's acerbic temperament. Now eighty-seven, Wynne still oversaw the Cosmopolitan Club's library archives. She had put my *Orlando* book on the Cos Club's library shelves.

I decided I wanted a marriage witness, too. The only person who knew the situation was the Doctor, and I was due to have dinner with him anyway. At the Greek restaurant, before I brought up the subject, he said, "You're lucky you know Charlotte. She's a smart cookie. She can do a lot for you." But then he sighed. "She gave you a vacation—I can't afford to go to Venice."

"That's too bad," I said.

He winked at me. "What's she got that I don't?"

I ignored his remark. Looking back, I find it strange that I asked the Doctor to be a witness. I suppose I wanted to bring two different sides of my life together, to make my history with the Doctor somehow fit with knowing Charlotte. And also, not sure of the marriage idea, I wanted the Doctor's approval.

The smoke from his Pall Mall cigarette kept wafting across our restaurant table toward me.

"Don't fall out of your chair when I say this," I said.

He pursed his lips, waiting.

"This is a secret, so don't tell anyone else. Charlotte and I are planning to get married. I wondered if you'd be my witness before a justice of the peace, in a few days."

He sucked in his cheeks, like a man who'd bitten into a lemon. He rubbed his thumb and index finger together, as though feeling the texture of a new substance to see if there was gold or fool's gold in it. "My dear friend," he said, "she can help you without getting married. She knows she won't last that long."

I sat back in my chair.

His brow furrowed. "The world might not look kindly on such a marriage."

The great champion of individual freedom saying this—that I should chicken out because of others' opinions?

I remembered what he'd told me about his own marriage, which had not lasted. Decades earlier, living in Westchester, he had met a woman who was impressed by his being a Park Avenue analyst. The woman didn't read books, but she had money, so he married her. Within six months he learned that his wife was a bigoted half-Jew who despised Jews. She had assumed he made lots of money, and she wanted to show off her "Park Avenue analyst" hubby at parties. The marriage was hopeless, and they divorced.

Now the Doctor said to me, "Women are different from us, you know. They get in the same boat with you. It's not like what you and I have—a friendship."

"But Charlotte and I *are* friends," I said.

He adjusted his glasses. "Anything's possible, I suppose."

He gave a shrug. "I hardly know Charlotte. I met her once, at your book signing. Whatever you decide, you know I'll support you."

Maybe I could help them know each other better, I thought. There was still time to see if they might get along. It was worth a try.

"I invite you to have dinner with us, with Charlotte and me, tomorrow night," I said.

"It would be an honor," he said.

* * *

I walked east through Central Park, enjoying the beauty of a crisp fall day. The marriage license was sleeping in Charlotte's sideboard drawer. Did we—did I—dare act on it? But first, tonight, was our dinner with the Doctor.

My feet hit the dirt horse trail, where riders on horses from the nearby stable on West 89th Street would occasionally gallop. Veering left through a stand of trees, I crossed a fine old wrought-iron bridge, re-planked so the footing was firm, to the jogging path circling the mile-and-five-eighths circumference of the Central Park Reservoir. I'd jogged it many times, once passing Jacqueline Onassis jogging in the other direction. A ten-foot-high link fence separated the path from the water. A news story came to mind. After drinking at a party, a teenager had climbed the fence for a nighttime swim across, but in the dark his head struck a stone divider just under the water's surface at the reservoir's center, and he drowned.

After walking around the reservoir, I was near the back of the Metropolitan Museum of Art, where a grassy slope had become a sunbathing field for citizens to enjoy the sun. The Egyptian temple inside the museum was visible through the windows above them. I continued, around the museum, and saw the street vendors in front. At a jewelry maker's table, I found a ring with bright red-and-blue enamel insets, costing only fifteen dollars. I knew Charlotte would like its colors and not care about its price, so I bought it: her wedding ring.

I walked east on 70th Street, past the fine old brownstone where Wynne lived, and then on to Charlotte's building. I would escort her to Shabu-Shabu, where the Doctor would meet us. I knew that she had agreed to the dinner only to please me.

At the restaurant, Noriko, the wife of the chef, led us to our favorite round table near the bar. The Doctor arrived in his formal suit and sat down next to Charlotte, across from me.

"Tonight's on me, my treat," I said.

The Doctor lit a cigarette. "Peter has told me that you smoke, also, Charlotte." He smiled, as though smoking was something important that they shared, before he went on. "When I was young, my father promised me a car if I did two things—to not smoke, and to join the family business, which was plastering ceilings. Charlotte, my father was an uneducated peasant."

"What's wrong with plastering ceilings?" said Charlotte.

"The bastard also offered me ten thousand dollars to start work for him. I refused, and I put myself through college."

Charlotte spit the lemon peel twist that had gotten into her mouth back into her martini glass. "I *didn't* go to college at all. I went into the auction business."

The Doctor rambled on, as though the conversation depended entirely on him. His father had condemned his love for the piano as being prissy, he said. "Charlotte, I was born into the wrong family. But I would rather eat a ham sandwich with a *friend* than a steak with someone I don't care about. As Rabbi Hillel said, 'If I am not for others, who am I for? If I am not for myself, who am I?'"

"Yes, of course," muttered Charlotte.

"Who do *you* admire, Charlotte?" he asked.

"Houdini! I saw him on stage escape from the water box."

"Houdini was a Jew," said the Doctor.

"I know," she said.

At this point Charlotte had to excuse herself to go to the ladies' room.

With her away, the Doctor looked at me with great gravity. "I'm not saying she isn't an impressive woman," he began.

"Spit it out. What *are* you saying?"

"She's expansive."

That was a key word in the Karen Horney books that the Doctor had all his patients read. To be expansive was to have a neurotic need to control others, or a situation, because one was insecure. In analysis I had learned that my mother was expansive, my father detached, and I was some combination of self-effacing with bouts of expansiveness. But, of course, it was never so simple as such categories implied.

"Charlotte's *not* expansive," I angrily told him. "She just knows what she likes and isn't afraid to show it."

His eyebrows arched, and he spread his hands. "My dear friend, tonight has shown me the obvious. The age difference is too big. You two have nothing in common—you've hardly said a word tonight."

How stupid could he be? I had been quiet only to let the two of them get to know each other better. And the only expansive person at the table, over-controlling the conversation, was the Doctor.

Just then Charlotte returned. We all ordered green tea ice creams for dessert. Charlotte was quiet, and I could see, in her face, that she was ready to leave. But the Doctor, as though determined to impress her, kept talking. "Peter's mother Sally was a more talented artist than his father. Poor Nick couldn't compete with her."

"You talk like he's dead!" Charlotte objected.

"Emotionally, he is."

"He is *not*. We read poetry together, and we will again!"

I wasn't sure how right the Doctor was about my father, but Charlotte was speaking from the heart.

After I paid the bill, outside on Second Avenue the Doctor hailed a taxi, and he was gone. Charlotte set a brisk pace walking home, but rounding her block's corner, she tripped over a flaw in the pavement and went down. I quickly helped her up. She seemed all right, her thick autumn coat having softened the fall. But after we entered her apartment, in the kitchen she showed me her wrist, which was swelling up. Face rigid, breathing too fast, she sat down and said softly, "I'm seeing in black and white."

Shock? Stroke? Heart attack? My mind raced as I dialed 911 on the rotary kitchen phone. I got someone, and I said that Charlotte, an older woman, had fallen, and gave our location.

"Wait," said Charlotte. She stood up and stepped to the garbage pail beside the stove, and threw up into it. "I'm okay now." I thanked 911 and hung up.

"I've heard of seeing in black and white," said Charlotte, "but I didn't know it was true."

Charlotte stood in front of the old Hotpoint refrigerator, and I noticed a tear creeping down her cheek. What effect had the tense evening and her fall had on her? Then, in a subdued voice, with an odd tone of defeat in it, she said, "Nobody dies with dignity."

I waited, not sure what to say.

She stared at me. "Poor Pat, it was so awful. I don't want to die alone in a horrible nursing home like he did."

Without having to think, and with absolute certainty, I told her, "You won't be alone. I'll be with you. I promise."

15

The Wedding Dream

Back at my apartment the next day, two pigeons cooed and crapped on my windowsill, on the other side of the glass. But I enjoyed their company, so I opened a different window for some air.

I was still shocked at how judgmental the Doctor had been at dinner. Maybe he was just plain jealous of Charlotte's closeness with me. I'd hoped he was more generous than that. Tomorrow was the last day that our marriage license was good.

My windowsill now had three pigeons on it, as I dialed Frank in Queens to ask if he would be my marriage witness.

"Peter, you've been drifting a long time, but maybe you've found something you're good at. I like Charlotte, so I'd be happy to be your witness."

I felt better.

Moments later, my phone rang, and it was my sister Beta, calling from Nevada. She started with just news, how she was writing an article about witches in Europe in the thirteenth and fourteenth century. She had a particular interest in female "outsiders" in the so-called Dark Ages, which she said were not as dark as they were commonly thought to be.

"Something else on your mind?" I asked.

"Well, John called me." She meant the Doctor, whom she and Charles called by his first name. "He sounded like he'd been drinking. He was upset." She spoke hesitantly. "He said something about a marriage idea."

I couldn't believe it.

"That's a secret," I said. "He wasn't supposed to tell anyone."

"He screwed up, then," said Beta.

Years ago the Doctor had told me that keeping a secret was crucial to being a real individual. He had used that idea when I had kept our secret—the sex.

"Not your fault," I told Beta.

"I guess he feels a responsibility to advise you, and he wasn't sure what to tell you."

So the sage had asked my own sister's opinion.

"What did you say?"

"I said that Charlotte, from her generation, might be more comfortable helping you if she and you were married. I have nothing against the idea. . . . It's a private matter between you and Charlotte."

"Thanks, Beta, I appreciate that."

After saying goodbye, I waited five minutes before calling him. The Doctor's voice sounded full of liquor as he said, "Thank you for the delightful dinner with Charlotte."

I admit that I set a trap to test his honesty, that I treated him like a snake. Casually I asked, "You haven't told anyone about the marriage idea, have you? Like I asked?"

"Of course not. You know me, I wouldn't do that."

"Drinking is no excuse."

"Now, Peter, don't be cruel. I don't think I said anything to anyone."

"I just talked to Beta. She knows."

"Will you forgive me?" he asked plaintively.

I hung up.

* * *

Charlotte sat bolt upright in bed. I felt I owed it to her, to let her know our secret was out. In a way it was my fault, for trusting the Doctor. Maybe I shouldn't have told her, but I felt that, as partners, we must be honest.

"Do you know how embarrassing this is for me?" Charlotte said.

I put my arm around her, but she pushed me away. When Charlotte got angry, she got angry. "I'll never forgive that horrible man!"

I sat down in a chair, not too near Charlotte on the bed. I'd realized something more completely: if we did marry, it would be very difficult to keep it a secret, in any case. For example, wouldn't Eric, her lawyer, have to know? More and more people would know.

And tomorrow was our last day; in the morning, would we go get married?

Charlotte had regained her composure, and we went into the living room to watch the six-thirty TV news with Tom Brokaw, her favorite newscaster. During a commercial, she said that Eric had called to remind her of her will changes, if she wanted any; and that she could call him until nine o'clock tonight. She wanted it settled tonight, whatever happened tomorrow.

From her past remarks, I knew how Charlotte loathed revising her will—she must have done it any number of times in her life already, and naturally it could be a distasteful task.

Concerning money, Charlotte would sometimes quote a Wordsworth poem: ". . . getting and spending, we lay waste our powers." She had long since come to see the power of sheer wealth with a dubious eye. She gave to many charities every Christmas, but she preferred giving to individuals whom she knew were in need.

Charlotte suddenly said, "I'm so tired. Please go look at my papers in the gray file cabinet, and tell me what I should do in my will. You decide." And she went to her room to rest and wait, closing her door.

She was asking me how much money I wanted.

Money and marriage. Didn't one choice affect the other? I felt confused, and couldn't clear my mind to think.

I fetched her investment statements, and spread them out under the two-tailed mermaid on the dining room table. I knew that millions from Morgan trusts would automatically go to all her extended family, so her surviving brother and various nieces and nephews would get plenty. But Charlotte also had a big account at Bank of America.

It's natural to want, another thing to deserve.

If we married, a surviving husband would get everything, because none of it could be taxed. If we did not marry, Charlotte's tax bracket dictated that half would go to the government. My mind and conscience were spinning. I was tied in knots.

I took a breather, and paced around the living room. I sat on the black couch where we'd first kissed. The portrait of Charlotte by Pat reminded me that she had helped him, too. Pat, she had told me, kept a metal box in his studio containing ten thousand dollars, just for eventualities. One thing was certain: Charlotte would rather be generous than selfish.

I got up, deciding to draw a picture of my dilemma. I often did this when my rational mind was stuck; I just drew to see what came out. As the mermaid looked on, without thinking I drew a big circle on a blank piece of paper. I waited, looking at it, before the circle reminded me of an alarm clock, so I sketched in numbers, an old-fashioned bell on top, and an hour hand approaching the eleventh hour. Still, I tried not to think too much.

Next the circle reminded me of an apple pie, so I drew lumps of warm apples under the dough, wavy lines of heat rising, and crimps at the pie's edges. How funny: I realized that there is such a thing as a financial "pie chart." I'd come full circle, but now with a clear mind.

I drew a line straight down the middle: half the pie was my answer.

Married or not, taxed or not, more than half going to me would be greedy. Less than half seemed self-effacing, not honest about my feelings.

The whole thing seemed not quite real, anyway, as I knocked on Charlotte's door.

"What did you decide?" she asked.

I told her.

"Good," she said.

We dialed up Eric.

* * *

On the wall of the guestroom I slept in hung a plaster bust of Voltaire that Pat had owned. According to Charlotte he had appreciated the story of Candide's never-ending tribulations and the absurdist, ironic optimism of "the best of all possible worlds."

I lay on my single bed. Maybe by morning, after turning and tossing all night with indecision, I would know how I felt about marriage. Oddly, though, I fell asleep right away.

In the morning my brain was like a frozen pond that refused to thaw. Sluggish as a hibernating frog, slow to move, I tried to face the day. But I found Charlotte, who usually slept late, already up having her coffee and eating a banana in the dining room. I got my coffee and sipped it beside her, as golden morning light cast the mermaid's dark shadow on the Venetian red wall.

As was her habit, Charlotte was reading the *New York Times* obituaries. A soprano, a World War II flying ace, and a famous hockey player had died.

"I had a dream last night," Charlotte said.

She described her dream. She was attending a wedding reception, and a young, beautiful blond bride was there. But the groom was absent. On a long table was lots of food, and Charlotte was hungry. Suddenly I appeared in the dream. I went to the table, and first I offered her a huge slab of ham. Charlotte dumped it on the floor. Then I offered her lobster claws with mayonnaise, but Charlotte threw them out the window. The third time, I offered her a delicious chicken salad, but Charlotte dumped it over my head.

I'm not sure why, but Charlotte's anger at me in her dream did not bother me. I was struck by how the dream resembled some kind of fairy tale that could express wisdom. At least she hadn't thrown *me* out the window, only the lobster.

Charlotte said, "I think we'd better not tie the knot."

I felt I should show some disappointment.

"Maybe you came to the same conclusion?" she asked.

No. I just hadn't had the courage to decide. I did know that marriage wasn't at the center of what we had, anyway.

"It doesn't mean we don't love each other," I said.

"We're still an odd couple," she said.

* * *

And that's how we didn't get married in 1989. But I had already made my most important vow, in Charlotte's kitchen.

PART 2

16

Charlotte's Family

Despite almost marrying, Charlotte and I still lived in separate apartments. Changing that would take a mishap, a bit of fate, and some disguised luck. In the meantime, as time went by, I was learning more about Charlotte's family.

I felt lucky that her surviving family lived far away from us, making it easier to keep our romance a secret. But meeting them would eventually help me know Charlotte. As with anyone, Charlotte's life and attitudes were influenced by family.

Her only surviving sibling, Charlie, was seventeen years younger than she and lived in Florida. Since they had not grown up together, and he was not as liberal-minded as his big sister, they simply weren't that close. But Charlotte did pay close attention to the younger generation—her brother's children and her deceased sister Nancy's children. She kept in touch with her nephews and nieces by phone. From what I saw, they all truly liked Charlotte. And it seemed safe to assume that, from a distance, they must see me as merely a young relative whom Charlotte had befriended.

From Charlotte's stories about her parents and her aunt and uncle (she often called them her "four parents"), I almost felt as though I knew them better than her living family. The first child of her generation, Charlotte had been raised like a beloved only child, in a mansion inhabited by all four doting "parents." I'd heard about the mansion in

New Rochelle, on Long Island Sound, but in 1990, with the help of a friend, we visited it.

Rick, a former saxophone teacher of mine (I dropped the instrument but gained a friend), offered to drive us to the mansion. Rick's Japanese girlfriend Akiko had taken an extraordinary liking to Charlotte. The four of us drove out so Charlotte could revisit her birthplace, which she hadn't been to in decades.

We parked in front of the Greentree Country Club, once the Church mansion, renovated by a Greek man as a venue for weddings, dances, and other events. The original tall, white columns still graced its front, and on its seaward side was the once-private beach on Long Island Sound. Charlotte's "four parents" would eventually move to separate, more impressive mansions in Mill Neck, Long Island, but that didn't happen until Charlotte was in her mid-twenties. (We would later visit the Church brothers' bequest of wetland property, the North Shore Wildlife Sanctuary in Mill Neck, with its boardwalks across refuges for fish and birds.)

The Greentree owner, thrilled to meet Charlotte, proudly invited us inside. We ascended one side of a double marble staircase to a landing, before the stairs branched again—one side to Charlotte's parents' quarters, the other to her aunt and uncle's. On the landing's wall, above a bench, hung a gaudy, ornate painting of angels and clouds. Looking confused, Charlotte asked, "Where's my window?"

The Greentree Club's huge new wing had blocked and eliminated the window, I told her.

Charlotte sat on the bench and told me why she missed the window.

At fourteen, she had sleepwalked, waking up barefoot and freezing in her nightgown, her nose pressed up against the window. In her dream she had wanted to get to Huckleberry Island, visible through the window, even though her mother had warned her that it was "a bad place, with a men's drinking club and God knows what else." Now, more than seventy years later, Charlotte repeated, "I *wanted* Huckleberry Island!"

Charlotte said, "I couldn't get there until I was seventeen, canoeing out with girlfriends. But by then there was nothing but deserted sidewalks, old trees, and a pathetic-looking, ruined beer castle of ragged stone."

Listening, I could suddenly imagine with more clarity Charlotte as a young girl full of curiosity and a lust for experience. I could connect who she had been then with Charlotte now, a woman with the appetite to become involved in her new adventure with me.

We toured the interior of the mansion, but it was mostly sanitized and robbed of its original character. We checked out the beach, now crowded with changing rooms and too many loungers. Charlotte was satisfied, and we left.

That night Charlotte showed me her family photo albums. I slowly turned the pages. There was my grandfather Pecks at three years old, dressed like a girl in a white nightgown. Charlotte's great-grandmother (my great, great aunt) stood in front of her house on Slocum's Island, later to become a public park a stone's throw from Detroit. There was Charlotte's father posing at ninety-five with a racquet on a tennis court to show that he still played the game. But most striking to me was a photo of Charlotte herself, age one: out of a frilly white gown and lacy cap, her eyes glowed with curiosity.

Between seeing the New Rochelle mansion and the photographs, now I could picture a typical day for her when she was about twelve years old. Maybe that age appealed to me because it had been my own happiest time, before childhood ended.

Here is what I envisioned:

In the summer, not having to go to school, Charlotte woke in her bedroom and ran down for a breakfast of oatmeal and a ripe orange, or eggs kept in the ice box, for which the ice man delivered a block of ice each week.

After breakfast, Charlotte fed her pets: an extravagantly colored parrot, the fat goldfish, a somewhat domesticated squirrel, and the legion of guinea pigs she named after books of the Bible, starting with Deuteronomy. For her pet chameleon's breakfast, she might swat a fly before letting the creature ride around on her blouse, like a brooch.

Going outside, she glanced at the magnificent sailing yacht floating in front of the neighbor's house—the Iselins were "very old money," Uncle Charlie had told her.

Charlotte then might meet with her girlfriends in the miniature house that Uncle Charlie had built for her. President and ringleader of their club, Charlotte had responsibilities. At their tea party, Charlotte solicited advice on how to get a live lobster to put in a neighbor boy's bed to scare him.

After lunch, served by the family cook, Charlotte kept her appointment posing for her father in his studio. Since her father paid his models, and she was his favorite, she had demanded a salary. Sitting still could be hard work, but she loved watching her father mix colors, and the smell of turpentine. She asked him, could they go butterfly hunting again soon?

After modeling, Charlotte would carefully crank up her "red bug" car (Uncle Charlie had warned her to be careful, that the crank could "take off your arm"), so she could drive around town, the people of New Rochelle waving to say hello.

In the waning afternoon, Charlotte climbed the rocks of her favorite inlet to see giant spider crabs twitching on the sand and a starfish on a rock pointing one leg out like a finger. If she was lucky, she might see dolphins close to shore—one had once brushed up against her swimming in the same water.

Charlotte's mother called her in for dinner: a standing rib roast. Her mother, slightly chubby and talkative, had marched for the women's vote, as had her Aunt Charlotte; so the two women might argue politics with the men. Uncle Charlie, working at Church and Dwight, talked some business. One thing the family agreed on: Charlotte got to drink the juice from the bottom of the rib roast. This because, when Charlotte had been sick, the family doctor had declared, "Your daughter is a carnivore, not a herbivore."

* * *

It was at the annual Church and Dwight stockholders' meeting, at the Asia Society on Manhattan's Upper East Side, that I first met members of Charlotte's living family. Her brother Charlie attended. He was so affably mild-mannered, bizarrely unlike his sister, that he was relatively uninteresting to me. But there I also met her favorite nephew, Scotty, son of deceased younger sister Nancy. Thickly muscled, bearded, very macho, he'd flown his own plane in from Virginia.

Talkative, robustly confident, Scotty made me wonder if I were meeting a younger, male version of Charlotte. Fifty-four-year-old Scotty was boastful but had an almost childlike, Southern gentlemanly charm. He doted on Charlotte, patiently listening to her espouse the wonders of baking soda—good for brushing your teeth, curing a sour stomach, or putting out a kitchen fire.

Scotty invited Charlotte and me to visit him and his girlfriend Jan in Virginia. A few weeks later, we boarded a train to Washington, DC, and from there Scotty drove us to his rural property. We saw his airplane hangar and a landing strip he had leveled himself with his earthmover. His house boasted tall white columns. Inside, I saw a full-length portrait of Charlotte as a young ice-skater, painted by her father. Scotty also had his grandfather's complete butterfly collection—Scotty had loved his grandfather, so Charlotte had allowed him to take what by rights was hers.

Scotty in his fitness room showed me how he could still lift three hundred pounds over his head. Then he unlocked his rare-gun collection and took out a pistol for target practice off his front porch. When I got my chance, surprisingly, I hit the tin can once, also. While all this went on, Charlotte was being taken care of by Scotty's live-in girlfriend, Jan.

At dinner Scotty shared his Borneo story. In his twenties, he had journeyed to Borneo with an English priest friend. In the jungle, Scotty ingratiated himself with a tribe by repairing, with his smelting skills, a rusty old rifle they had found. On the ensuing wild boar hunt, a boar charged Scotty, and he aimed the repaired rifle, which did a terrifying, dramatic "slow burn" before it finally went off, dropping the boar literally at Scotty's feet. As reward for his bravery, the chief invited Scotty to sleep with his daughter. He did. But as the morning light filled the hut he slept in, Scotty noticed that there was an array of shrunken human heads decorating the interior. Scotty and the priest escaped in a canoe.

Well, that was pretty impressive, to me.

The best I could do to compete with that was to draw a quick portrait of Charlotte at the dinner table. My pen kept misfiring, but everyone politely said the portrait was good.

The next morning Scotty showed us his earthmover. In its big shovel he had placed a mattress. Charlotte and I lay, head to foot, on the mattress as Scotty gave us a tour of the farm. Lifted above a stone wall, we were cascaded by pink tree blossoms.

Scotty's enthusiasm was exhausting, but he wasn't done. Thirty years earlier, he had taken Charlotte on a one-hundred-mile-per-hour car ride, and in that spirit he invited her on his motorcycle now. Eighty-nine-year-old Charlotte put on a big red helmet and got on the bike behind her nephew, and they disappeared down the road. After the ride Charlotte smiled bravely but walked a bit bowlegged—she later told me that spreading her thighs wide enough for the bike had been "excruciating."

It was a relief that night to meet Scotty's sister Marybeth, who had no need to dominate. She was warm and friendly, and we liked each other immediately. Marybeth had two daughters, and Charlotte was paying for one of them to attend a private school.

The next day, when we got back to New York, Charlotte pointed at her oval desk. "Six-year-old Scotty peed on that desk," she said. And then I heard the background of how that had happened. Scotty and Marybeth's mother, Nancy, had imitated Charlotte but did not have her older sister's stable nature or healthy constitution. Nancy tried to kill herself by swallowing batteries. While she recuperated in the hospital for a month, Charlotte cared for little Scotty and Marybeth. That's when Scotty had peed on the oval desk. Charlotte went on, "If anyone tells me I don't know about taking care of children, I give them what for, because Scotty and Marybeth were a handful."

I never heard any evidence that Charlotte regretted not having her own children. She freely admitted, to anyone, that she had had three abortions. She told me that she wouldn't have been a good mother, but I don't know why she said that. By the time she met Pat, maybe the best opportunity, Charlotte was already in her mid-forties. I never pursued the subject further. It did occur to me that if she had had children, she might not have been so interested in me.

I'm jumping ahead here but must give Scotty his due. Years after our visit to Virginia, he honestly explained to me why he "wore so much armor," as he put it, meaning his own blustery persona. He didn't mention his unstable, suicidal mother but did describe his father. When Scotty was a child, his journalist father, back from adventures in South America, would rise from his desk and, for no reason, smack Scotty across the room. His father taught him to shoot and hunt, but that didn't make up for the abuse, and when Scotty was a teenager, he tried to attack his father with a knife. For that he was briefly institutionalized, which went on his record. Ever after, even though transformed into a good citizen, Scotty had to relive and explain his incarceration to renew his pilot's license.

Charlotte loved Scotty and Marybeth, and they loved her. Charlotte no doubt gave them some feeling of having a more dependable family.

* * *

Charlotte also did her best to be good to her brother Charlie's children. Son Johny had been a sniper in Vietnam, so Charlotte regularly mailed him "care packages" of fine foods. When Johny came to New York, he mentioned to me how much her packages had meant to him. With a smile he said that only one item had not appealed to him and his Vietnam buddies: the oysters.

Charlie's other son, Freddy, was a born-again Christian in Utah. Freddy often called Charlotte on the phone, and he mailed her gift jars of his garden-grown vegetables. Charlotte patiently listened to his harangues about religion.

As to Charlie's daughter, Alice, Charlotte told me a story. When Alice was a little girl, her parents loved to put on huge, lavish parties in Florida. At one of those parties, Charlotte searched for Alice and found her high on a balustrade, hiding. Pointing down at the crowd, shy Alice confided to her aunt, "too many peoples."

When they learned about it, Alice's parents banished her from the house because she was gay. Decades later Alice resurfaced and reconciled with Charlie, and shortly after that she flew to New York to visit Charlotte, whom she had always liked. I was in the room when Alice talked about her career as an airline stewardess and described her longtime female partner. Alice knew that Charlotte would bear no prejudice.

17

A Break That Binds

In late summer of 1990, an accident brought Charlotte and me closer together, making us true companions.

I was borrowing the extra car in Kent to drive to Woodstock. Before leaving, I phoned Charlotte about my arrival time, and I mentioned a weather report predicting thunderstorms headed her way in the Hudson Valley.

Saying she might still be at a concert when I arrived, and not wanting me to get wet, she said to wait on the phone so she would run to ask her handyman John, about to go to lunch, to leave the house unlocked for me.

I waited, but Charlotte never came back to the phone. Instead John spoke. "I'm afraid Mrs. Collins has fallen on the patio stones and can't get up."

"Call 911," I said.

To save me from a few drops of rain, Charlotte had literally run across the uneven patio stones to catch John.

I drove to Kingston Hospital, near Woodstock, where the ambulance had taken Charlotte. Jan and Ed were in the room where she lay with a broken hip. A translucent green mask with a hose like an elephant's trunk covered her face, making a hissing sound.

"Don't let the mask freak you, man. It's for oxygen," Ed said.

A surgeon came in and explained that, worse than the hip, Charlotte had a blood clot that might move to her heart and kill her. So she must be on a blood thinner for a full week before he could operate on her hip.

He noticed Jan writing on a pad. "If you take notes, I won't continue." Jan frowned. The surgeon left the room.

"Damn hospital watching their own asses," commented Ed.

Seeing Charlotte so helpless made me lightheaded, so I had to sit down. The possibility of her dying had never really occurred to me before. Ed put a hand on my shoulder, and Jan said that, of the three of us, I should be the one to tell Charlotte the situation. I snapped out of my shock enough to function.

I leaned over Charlotte, close to her face, and said that she must wait a week before her operation. She managed to put her hand up to her mask, lift it off, and say with conviction, "No, I want to go to *New York Hospital.*"

Jan said we needed a second opinion, so we went down the hall to look for another doctor, and luckily found one. This doctor had been trained in India. He patiently listened and said, "At her age she knows herself best. I agree with her." He confided that some Kingston doctors tried to keep patients for themselves because they envied the New York specialists. But he would authorize Charlotte to leave.

Through a friend, Jan contacted a New York Hospital surgeon who would take responsibility for Charlotte and could operate as soon as she arrived. Early the next morning I rode with Charlotte in the ambulance to Manhattan.

The New York surgeon put a tiny "umbrella" screen into Charlotte's artery to block the clot, and fixed her hip with a plate and a screw. I knew Charlotte was okay when, only a few hours later, I overheard her excitedly tell a nurse, "In the elevator, after I woke up, I saw the handsomest doctor in the world! He had curly blond hair like an angel and a perfect nose." The nurse laughed. She said all the nurses were crazy for Dr. Montgomery.

I visited Charlotte every day. She liked the hospital's Greek salad, and I often ate some of her other food.

On one of those days, she described a dream she'd had. She was in a pup tent in Africa. Her Uncle Charlie brought her delicious fruits—mangos, kumquats, persimmons, and tangerines. Cool air blew in through the tent flap, and a Siberian tiger stuck his head in and licked Charlotte's face. I figured that her nighttime oxygen mask might explain her dream's cool breeze. The rest of the dream was more real than one might think: after all, her uncle and aunt had safaried in Africa and brought home food treats and exotic pets for their niece.

In a week Charlotte was discharged.

Back in her apartment, Charlotte said to me that she had been surprised how often I had visited her in the hospital, not missing a day. Surprised? I hadn't even thought about it—I'd just been drawn to her. It had been a natural, good feeling.

In my life I had so often been confused between what I should do and what I really wanted to do. Sometimes I couldn't tell the difference. Despite my parents lapsing from two religions—Catholicism and Christian Science—I had been imbued with a hyper moral sense of how I was supposed to behave. For example, I should never, ever lie, even a "white lie." But the inner pressure of trying to be that perfect was impossible, so I ended up avoiding much of life, being afraid to fail. What I'm trying to say is simply that finally, in my concern for Charlotte, I found a pure motive. Loving her was becoming the clearest fact in my life.

A visiting nurse and home health aides came during the days, but Charlotte wanted only me at night. So this was how we began living together, even while I still had my West Side apartment.

Charlotte would, now and then, hyperventilate. We had a medical inhaler at hand, but at night I became terrified that she might have an attack or just stop breathing. I would wake up every hour or two and tiptoe in to squat by her bed to see the outline of her chest against the city-lit window. Yes, motion, she was breathing. Relieved, I'd return to bed, only to be drawn back, like a planet in the orbit of Charlotte.

Worrisome also was Charlotte's irregularly fast heartbeat—quick as a bird's. She had to take a little yellow Lanoxin pill each morning and a baby aspirin to smooth her blood.

She was both an excellent and a bad patient, sometimes refusing the nurse's instructions. Told she must always sit on a plastic bench to take a bath (not a real bath at all), she asked me to help her step into the tub so she could lay down full length for a good, hot soak. I remembered her shyness in Maine, when she held up a washcloth to hide herself. Now, in the bright bathroom light, she let me see all of her. With a washcloth I scrubbed her back.

Charlotte was soon walking around her apartment, and using her hospital-issue cane only when she went out. As we walked to lunch at Shabu-Shabu, she claimed her cane was a good weapon if anyone ever bothered her.

We went to the opera. Waiting for a bus, she lit up her Camel to speed the bus's arrival. We were back to normal life. When I felt a soft pressure on my right foot, I looked down to see Charlotte's rubber-tipped cane resting on my shoe. It felt like the paw of a dog or cat, resting there with that natural trust. I nudged Charlotte to look down, and we both laughed at this little new sign of how close we had become.

* * *

Living with Charlotte would usher in an inevitable change, even if at first I thought I should resist it. I mean in my finances. I was teaching two composition courses for a pittance, while living with a rich woman.

Completing my English PhD had begun to feel pointless except as a way to get better teaching. For even though I enjoyed writing academic papers, I was no committed scholar. It was only painting or creative writing that truly excited me. Original art, to my mind, was the raw data of my world. And Charlotte knew this about me.

But I would never ask Charlotte to support me. I did not want to feel like a quitter at making my own living.

Charlotte sensed my dilemma. One day she suggested that I might work as her "personal secretary." I suspected that she was actually trying to find a way to share her money with me.

We tried it on a trial basis.

I'd imagined that I might, as her secretary, keep a sharp eye on her investments and write out checks for her to sign. But little of that kind of work was needed. Instead I found myself helping her go through the long-neglected stuffed and forgotten drawers of her oval desk. I took out a single deep drawer and carried it over to the couch so we could sift through the contents. We found all manner of old Christmas cards, ancient postcards, stamps, coins, art show announcements, wadded up Kleenex, bus schedules— all kinds of detritus. A few finds were interesting, like Pat's FREE IRELAND and IRA buttons, and a cache of love letters from Bunny. But here was the rub: the exceedingly slow pace of Charlotte's decision making about what to keep, and how to organize what she kept, was excruciating for me. I started again to feel like a butler or servant, as I had in Maine bringing hot water for Charlotte's bath. I'd rather have excavated Charlotte's desk for free. I wanted my work to carry some sense of stature.

When Charlotte wrote me a fifty-dollar check for the oval desk work, the absurdity of the situation became obvious to both of us. I was already using Charlotte's ATM card for our daily expenses (she hated struggling with that newfangled card). With her money I bought all our groceries and paid for all our dinners out.

I should mention something here. We have all heard about awful situations where a trusted younger person takes financial advantage of a gullible or incompetent older person. From my new vantage point, I could almost imagine how such a thing could take place. But it could never happen with us, because Charlotte was smart, independent, and no fool, and I am too honest.

It just made sense for us to share her money.

With Charlotte's blessing, at the end of the semester, I stopped teaching. By taking one more course and writing a thesis, I salvaged a master's degree in something called "Independent Studies." Meanwhile, the only reason I'd been going to my West Side apartment was to paint. So that I could work more conveniently close to her in my own space, Charlotte signed as guarantor for my new small studio on East 74th Street.

I now had a lifestyle similar to my parents', so I damned well better paint some good pictures. Or I wouldn't be able to live with myself.

18

You're Living Too Old

In Woodstock that summer, I landed an "Emerging Artists" show at the Woodstock Art Association. Their permanent collection included works by well-known artists such as Milton Avery and Philip Guston. Pat's best painting, entitled *VJ Day*, was enshrined there. The Association was a step up for me. I avoided the thought that Charlotte's name, on a plaque as a contributor to the Association, had influenced the jury.

The opening attracted Charlotte's Woodstock friends, people I knew in Kent, and, fortunately, strangers. And it brought my father.

My father looked happy and proud. And he showed no annoyance that one of my paintings was an unflattering image of him. I had painted him in oil, using an old photograph taken on a family camping trip when I was about five. My father sits on a rock, his skin the color of beaten bronze in the bright sunlight, his eyelids shut tight. It wasn't that he blinked at the wrong instant for a photo. No, he looks in psychic pain, isolated and unreachable, totally occupied with his own inner self. I imagine he was depressed when the photo was taken, having been dragged into camping by my mother. That was in the '50s, when families were expected to take happy, classic camping trips. My mother had taken me and my sister Beta to gather lake snails, which we cooked over our fire as an appetizer before dinner.

At the opening Charlotte tried to nudge her friend Janet to buy a painting. They were looking at *Seed and Husk*, a picture in which a baby happily holds a paintbrush, even though he is imprisoned in a giant, adult male head.

"It makes no sense to me," said Janet.

"It's surrealism, for God's sake," said Charlotte.

A month later the show closed, without my selling a single painting. That night, with all my paintings back in Charlotte's house, stacked in Pat's old studio room, I drank some gin.

Drink in hand, I stared at my paintings and thought of them as pathetic, flat, dead rectangles of frozen time. I imagined them as headstones in my own graveyard. Melodramatically, I tried to escape into an artistic theory that could explain my depression, my show's failure. I remembered a famous Durer print entitled *Melencholia*, and another Durer print that illustrated, in side view, the motionless lines of classic perspective. I figured that, by using traditional perspective, as though the artist sees with only a single, unmoving eye, I had frozen not only what I saw but also myself in space and time. My approach to art was immobilizing me as a person.

Drunk on gin, I took a one-sided razor blade that I used to clean my glass palette and moved toward my work . . . I chose the one of my father. I put the sharp corner of the blade to the image of one of his unseeing, closed eyes, and I sliced through the canvas, cutting in widening circles until the entire canvas collapsed.

Then I went out to the kitchen, where Charlotte was sitting, and said to her, "The only reason I got that show is because you gave money to the Association."

"Don't denigrate yourself!" she said. "*All* artists need connections. Now I'm tired and have to go to bed."

Shortly after that, in bed together, I confessed to her that I'd slashed the painting of my father.

She cringed. "That's awful!"

"It was a release. I painted it—I can destroy it."

Whimpering, her body shook.

How could she understand that I had my own private survival

strategies, which had a logic all their own? My self-hate had to be meted out in smaller, punitive doses—like slashing a painting—to siphon off the poison, to avoid even worse catastrophe. As she lay quiet, discouraged, I saw my own angry thoughts like electricity weaving radioactive patterns in the dark air above us. Beautifully masochistic pictures, abstract in their purity. It was only after several minutes—or longer?—that the process reached a crescendo and my body relaxed.

I suddenly knew how badly I'd treated Charlotte. She had dedicated herself to my show, supporting me completely. In destroying the painting, I had hurt her.

"Maybe I can repair the picture?" I said.

"Impossible," she replied.

She was right. It would take an art restoration miracle to repair that picture.

At least I'd calmed down. Charlotte, it must be said, was a very strong person. With her I could express even the worst of my feelings, and even when it hurt her badly, she was capable of forgiving me.

I suspect that she already knew what I needed to learn: that my anger at my father was all mixed up with my anger at myself, and I needed to learn the difference.

Then I touched Charlotte and she touched me, and both wanting to feel better, we made love.

* * *

About a week after my show closed, Charlotte and I drove into Woodstock for a snack and shopping. I was still obsessed with my show's failure. We parked and walked to the tiny triangular park in the center of town. There the scene was reminiscent of the '60s, young people mixing with old hippies. Above us, a pair of red sneakers hung by tied laces on a telephone wire.

While Charlotte waited on a bench, I went to get us hot dogs. Traffic clogged Tinker Street, Woodstock's main drag, so I waited and scampered across. I bought the dogs—hers with mustard, mine with ketchup—and re-crossed Tinker. I handed Charlotte her lunch, but ketchup from my hot dog had leaked all over the napkins.

"If you don't mind, go back and get fresh napkins," said Charlotte.

Couldn't she just use a Kleenex? Her fastidiousness could drive a person crazy. Back I went, across the street, for napkins.

We ate in silence between us, as a teenager on a nearby bench played his guitar and a couple of nubile girls worshipped him, strumming and yelping. I couldn't resist looking at one of the girl's thighs, circled by cut-off jeans.

I hadn't touched the body of a female younger than eighty-eight in four years.

"Time to grocery shop," said Charlotte.

Glumly I asked, "What is your pleasure for dinner?"

"Fish, if it's fresh. Remember to lift the awful plastic to smell the fish to make sure it's fresh."

"I *always* smell it for you."

I sometimes resented Charlotte's rules. I was shy about lifting the plastic that covered wrapped fish, or if there were fish out in a counter, asking to let me smell it.

"Nose!" said Charlotte. "Very important."

"Your wish is my command."

Charlotte threw her crumpled-up hot dog foil toward a trash basket, and missed. I grunted before getting up to put it in the basket. "Sometimes living with you is hard sledding," said Charlotte.

Sledding. Of course in the beginning of the century, she had been on sleigh rides drawn by horses. Her long view on life could get wearisome to contemplate.

We sat in mutual silence, not getting along at all. I thought, If only I'd sold one painting, I would feel better now. I could not stop thinking of my show's failure.

"Hey, you!" came a voice from behind us.

It was Ed Doyle, all dressed up in a colorful Hawaiian shirt, white linen pants, and red tennis sneakers. "This is my retro look," he said.

Tall and dapper, he looked down at us. "I'm on a beer run, man," he said to me, but not to Charlotte. "Our landlords are away, so we're having a pool party. Come quick or you'll miss all the fun. Babes in the pool, man."

Charlotte could hear that Ed was inviting only me, not her, but she didn't object.

I told him I'd try to make it. He ran off.

"Take the car, *quick*, or you'll miss the party," said Charlotte. "I'll walk home by myself."

That was ridiculous. I couldn't let her walk home.

"I'll cook my own dinner from leftovers," she said.

My sense of duty was stronger than her gambit. We went back to the car and drove to the Grand Union. She waited in the car, as I tried to find sure-fire fresh fish, but couldn't. So I got baby lamb chops, asparagus, and little red potatoes. When I got back in the car, Charlotte ominously slid an index finger over her lips, like a small girl zipping them shut. She was pissed.

At the house, as I put the food in the refrigerator, Charlotte made a martini—only one. "You go to the party," she said.

With my bathing suit on under my pants, I drove faster than usual. It was a compliment that Ed had invited me, and he was right to guess that I sometimes craved meeting younger women. And Ed had become a good friend, so I didn't want to snub him. After trying his video camera, I had bought my own, and designed what I called my "video drawing table." Using his carpentry skills, Ed had transformed my idea into reality. On my table's Plexiglas top, on translucent paper lit by side-mounted lights, I could draw pictures in time, like video jazz. I recorded the process with a camera mounted underneath, shooting through a mirror, so words I might write would be readable. Video satisfied my narrative urge as still pictures couldn't.

As I pulled into Ed's driveway, a last car of guests left. I was too late. From his porch, Ed yelled, "There's always a straggler."

"Circumstances conspired," I answered.

"C'mon, kid," he motioned me out of my car. "You missed the party, but we can take a dip."

We walked through a small stand of scraggly fir trees to the pool, owned by the interior decorators. Ed made a flat dive into the water while I stripped down to my suit, and stepped onto the diving board. The pool below me was a purple-tiled eggplant shape. I leaped and plunged, and rose in a swirl of bubbles.

Standing in the shallow end, Ed watched me with an odd expression on his face, more smirk than smile.

"Want my personal opinion?" he said.

I nodded, having no idea what he was talking about.

"Art comes from life, my man. You're stale. You need stimulation."

Was he talking about my not having sold a painting? No, his criticism was more than that.

"You missed some beautiful babes at this party." Snapping the wet waistband of his bathing suit with his thumbs, he showed off his lean midsection, seeming to make fun of the little gut I'd started around my own middle. "I wanted to get you out with a younger crowd, but you blew it."

He was right on that.

"Jan gets pissed when I chase the young ladies, but so what? Charlotte's cool and all—but face it man, she's already had her life. You should hang with people your own age."

"I have friends my age," I defended myself. I had Frank, a few old friends in Kent, a grad school friend or two.

"You're living too old, man."

It was like being punched.

"It was time to tell you," Ed went on. "You're isolated, socially paranoid. It's depressing."

I climbed out of the pool. I was so angry that I wanted to hit him back. Where did he get the right to tell me how to live?

"No, Ed—*you're* the one who's depressing *me*." And I left.

But as I drove, Ed's words were sinking in. I was too isolated, maybe even socially paranoid. I parked in the turnaround outside Charlotte's, but rather than go inside, I sat on the iron bench near her front door, and smoked a couple of cigarettes. Not yet a true smoker, I inhaled deep: to hell with health.

I thought, *Charlotte doesn't know I'm back,* so I could drive into town right now, go to a bar and look for a young woman.

But then I heard the phone ring inside the house, and Charlotte didn't answer it. Whether out of duty, or my not really wanting or daring to go to a bar, I went inside and picked up the phone. "Hello?"

"Peter, I'm glad I caught you," said the Doctor. "I wouldn't bother you there, but I have good news." News about himself, landing a new patient, or winning some lottery money? No, it was news for me.

He'd told Bradley, the artist who did his portrait, about my show, and Bradley had seen it, and he wanted to buy a painting, my *Seed and Husk*. But I must deliver it to him in the city.

My show was saved! In a split second, my mood went from pain to relief, even to joy.

I found Charlotte sound asleep in her room. In the center of the floor was one of her slippers. Picking it up, I saw a big, smashed wolf spider. Slaying it must have exhausted her. Her fear of spiders could have started when, as a child, she'd played in her attic with tiny black spiders with red spots on their bellies, that Uncle Charlie warned her were black widows.

She woke. I told her about my sale. Happy and relieved for me, she said to take the painting to New York before the buyer changed his mind.

19

Rewards of Success

I carried *Seed and Husk,* wrapped in plastic, onto a bus bound for Manhattan. With one of its stretchers against my knee, the canvas took up two seats. My one sale had magically banished my fear that I had no talent. It even hinted that I might be extraordinarily gifted— I was too happy not to daydream about the possibilities.

Bradley knew lots of people with money, even famous people like Leontyne Price, the opera singer, whose portrait he had painted. He gave lavish parties where such people might see my work. Even as the bus bogged down in traffic before entering the Lincoln Tunnel into Manhattan, my grand mood persisted.

Outside on Eighth Avenue, a stiff breeze almost blew the painting out of my hands, so I held its edge with one hand—better to let the air play with it than to fight the wind. Fortunately, it fit into the back seat of a taxi. At Christopher Street, downtown, I got out and sailed the picture, tacking it into the wind, to Bradley's brownstone.

Answering his door, Bradley appeared, dressed in a loose white cotton shirt and pants, a white silk cravat around his neck. He looked like an urban Lawrence of Arabia.

"Unwrap it and put it there." He pointed to a wall of his large darkened living room with heavily draperied alcove windows. An elaborate glass chandelier hung from the ceiling. I felt like I had entered an Edgar Allen Poe story.

Without a word, with his checkbook in hand, Bradley sat down at a desk and asked to be reminded of the price. I thought I should make it a thousand, not the fifteen hundred it would have cost him at the show, a third going to the Association.

"Wait, wasn't it more?" said Bradley.

I explained.

"Don't be a child." He ripped up the check he'd started, to write another. "Charge me the full price." He handed me the new check.

In my fantasy I had imagined us taking some time, two artists talking about art. But Bradley quickly ushered me to the door, back to the street. "Sorry to rush you," he explained, "but I have work to do. The Atheneum in Hartford is giving me a show— saving my life." He shut his door.

Saving his life?

Whatever he meant, I had sold a picture. I started uptown, as I had arranged to meet the Doctor for dinner. I owed him that much for making the connection.

We sat down in a moderately priced Italian restaurant, and I learned the reason for Bradley's odd remark. Why hadn't the Doctor told me earlier that Bradley had throat cancer, so wore the cravat to hide his neck? Doctors had told him he did not have long to live. Now his remark made sense: the Atheneum's invitation to show had buoyed his will to survive longer, or perhaps he'd even taken it as a sign that he would not die at all.

"Bradley thinks he knows exactly what your painting is about," the Doctor added. "Rebirth into some kind of afterlife." But my *Seed and Husk* was only about a child, alive in the present, trapped in the adult head. It was merely psychological symbolism, about my own state of mind.

"Bradley's no dope, Peter," said the Doctor. "He says you've made great progress in your painting. You know we all want to kill our fathers, and now you've outdone Nick."

I didn't argue the point. I was there to thank the Doctor, and I paid for our dinner.

Then I took a bus north on Broadway, all the way to 91st Street, to a bar I knew that was called The Library. I was celebrating my sale, on vacation from the rest of my life. Sitting at the bar, I looked for a pretty young woman I might talk to, but on a Tuesday night, still early, I saw none. After a couple of drinks, I left to walk down Broadway toward my old apartment, where I had a month left on my lease. I walked by a woman in a miniskirt who asked, "Going out?"

I kept walking before I couldn't resist, stopping to look back at the hooker. Years ago, I had given in to such temptation a few times, but then it was about lust, and loneliness. I'd not been proud of it, but it was no sin, either. This time felt entirely different—I had sold a painting, so I deserved a celebration.

The girl, maybe twenty, had a rosy, clean-scrubbed face and curly blond hair. "My name's Debby. I'm kinda new at this," she said as we walked. Her price was $100 to go to my place.

In my apartment, I paid her right away so she wouldn't have to worry about that. I didn't like the idea of paying for sex, so I needed some actual warmth and friendliness between us. I asked Debby if I could sketch her while we talked, and she was flattered, never having sat for a portrait before. She said she was from Colorado, where her father was a policeman. "He'd die if he knew I'm doing this. I'm saving money to go to John Jay College, to become a criminal profiler."

She liked my sketch, so I gave it to her. After that she took off her clothes, and I did another, quicker portrait for me to keep. First she started with her mouth on me, before she took out a condom. It was good, for what it was. As she dressed, she said she'd see me again. I knew she wouldn't.

After four years, I'd finally cheated on Charlotte.

I did feel some guilt, but at least I had been careful. There was no sense ever telling Charlotte, since it would only hurt her. In the morning I took the bus back to Woodstock.

I never did tell Charlotte about the hooker, but in a careless moment over dinner, I possibly did worse, by stupidly sharing what Ed had told me at the pool the week before—his accusation that I was "living too old."

"Who is *Ed* to criticize you? I'll tell *him* what for!" she said with anger.

"Please, don't say anything," I begged, not wanting Ed to think I was hiding behind Charlotte's skirts.

I thought her anger might blow over, but that evening, from the kitchen, I overheard her talking on the phone with Jan. "Ed shouldn't have said that to Peter!" Then, "He's jealous of Peter's talent!"

Then I overheard what was perhaps the greater cause of Charlotte's temper. "Why wasn't I invited to the *party?*" she demanded. Pause. "No, Jan, I would *not* have fallen into the pool. You worry too much about me."

So safety had been Jan's reason, if not Ed's.

And apparently, Jan did not mind Charlotte criticizing Ed, because their conversation lightened, turning to a more pleasant subject. "Oh yes, Chippendale's, let's do it again soon," said Charlotte. Some time earlier, the two of them had gone to the Manhattan club with its near-naked male strippers. I'd heard about their girls' night out, when a handsome dancer had come down off the bar to give Charlotte a kiss.

"I love you, too," Charlotte said, before she hung up.

They had a beautiful friendship, those two.

20

My Father's Eyes

That same week my father telephoned to tell me that he had meant to visit Woodstock before my show closed, but he had been under the weather with a persistent backache. He wanted to buy one of my paintings.

He asked if I could drive to Kent, so we could discuss which painting he would buy. I said yes.

Only after hanging up did I panic: what if he wanted the painting of him that I had destroyed with a razor blade? Could I lie, say that I had sold it instead of *Seed and Husk?*

Next day, I drove across the Hudson River to Route 199, which curves like a snake through the New England landscape. Worrying about which painting he might want sapped any pleasure I might have gotten from seeing a red barn, cows, horses, or a scummy green pond perfect for frogs. By the time I got to Skiff Mountain, the silo on my father's property rose like an accusing finger in the air.

As he let me in the back door, my father wore his dark glasses. He suggested we have a drink. We sat in front of the two-hundred-year-old windows where he and my mother had talked about art, books, and psychology. Blair, the longhaired black-and-white cat, tried to jump onto his lap, but he shooed her away. He lit up a True cigarette.

"I might as well enjoy smoking," he said, "until I learn otherwise."

He coughed. "I didn't want to tell you on the phone, but an X-ray shows a spot on my lung."

The X-ray had been routinely taken before a recent eyelid procedure. A biopsy had already been done, and a nearby oncologist would give his diagnosis to my father tomorrow morning. Would I accompany him to the oncologist? Of course I would, I told my father.

And my father's new renter, now living in his studio, would join us. Ann Callahan was a longtime family friend who herself had survived lung cancer and a brain tumor. She would take the time off from her job running a Head Start program.

That settled, I noticed a Wallace Stevens poetry volume on the coffee table. It was opened to a long poem entitled *Notes Toward a Supreme Fiction*. Having read it in graduate school, and figuring that my father wanted some distraction, I quoted aloud a line that I remembered.

"Soldier, there is a war between the mind and sky."

"You know Stevens?" My father asked.

"A little."

We discussed the line I had quoted. My father saw the "soldier" as literally a soldier of World War II. But I saw the poem's war as also metaphorical, so the soldier could be any of us, in the war of life. I reminded my father about the funeral director, asking if my mother was a "veteran," and how we'd all laughed because she was not a veteran in the narrow sense.

My father took off his dark glasses. I saw his gray-blue eyes. "You may have a point there," he said. "I didn't know you took poetry so seriously."

I thought, How odd that we had never talked about poetry before now.

But then, how much did we really share? He had only commented once on my mysterious closeness with Charlotte, shyly suggesting that I was looking for "unconditional love." I was sure that he had no idea of the physical side of it. In my view there were always conditions to love. My father was such a purist, an idealist. No doubt his purity of vision was one reason he had not satisfied my mother in the bedroom, driving her to find other men. My father had probably never had sex with any other woman besides my mother in his entire life.

But at this moment, we were having a good time talking. Now he shyly told me what seemed a secret. "I've started writing poetry again," he said. "Maybe sometime I could show you some."

But for the time being, there was dinner.

He'd bought steak and asparagus but had forgotten to buy potatoes, he said. How about rice, I suggested. He had never, in his life, cooked rice. So I cooked it.

As we ate, we were two men in a house full of paintings—his, my mother's, and a few by me—trying to make conversation.

He cleared his throat. "Peter, something's been on my mind. At your opening I was struck by how, in your painting of me, my eyes are closed."

The eyes I'd slashed.

"It's not easy for me to say these things, but I want you to know that my eyes are open now. I see things, and I see *you* more clearly."

The fork in his hand was shaking. I had to give him credit. In bridging the gap between us, he had made the most important move.

* * *

Early next morning, I sat by myself on the back porch and stared past the stand of four tall pines and two old birches to the field now used for horses, but where cows had munched grass when I was a kid. I used to wander with my collie dog Skiff all over the ninety-five acres. Friends Paul and Jed and I made the huge barn and companion sheds into our own "Wild West Town," using an old spinning wheel as our roulette wheel. We waded in the nearby shallow pond, and a rock I stepped on turned out to be a snapping turtle. We boys got so mucky wading in the mud that, when we walked back to the house, my mother mistook us for three strange black boys somehow on the property. She had loved telling that story at cocktail parties.

Ann Callahan, sixtyish and thin, appeared on the other side of the porch's screen, ready for our trip to the oncologist. By now my father was up. I drove him, Ann following in her car. The idea was that I would continue on back to Woodstock after the meeting.

The doctor's waiting room had gauzy beige curtains that billowed slightly from the half-open windows, as though we had entered the chest of a giant patient trying to breathe. We sat and waited.

After we went into the oncologist's office, the doctor came in, a handsome middle-aged man whose black hair was perfectly parted. He looked down at a folder and said, "It's not good news, Nick. It's lung cancer, of the large cell variety."

He recommended radiation first, then chemotherapy.

Still composed, but in a voice an octave too high, my father asked, "What are you saying?"

"I have a lot of experience with this, Nick. I'd estimate you have between six months and a year. I'm sorry, it's inoperable."

"Inoperable," repeated my father. Then, doing something I would never forget, he stood and stepped carefully to the middle of the concentric, colored circles of the rug. Saying, "I think I'm going to faint," he lowered himself to sit, then lay back, and fainted. Later, Ann would tell me, "I never saw such a graceful, civilized faint."

As we left, my father said he understood that I was expected back at Charlotte's, that he was content to ride home with Ann. He was in good hands with her, he said. Ann whispered to me, "Call me, we'll talk."

Driving, I tried to absorb the diagnosis but felt dazed. One short sob erupted in me, but otherwise I remained oddly detached, as though sleeping and incapable of waking up. After parking in Charlotte's driveway, I told her the news.

"It's so sad, so awful," Charlotte said, her eyes filling with tears.

21

Reconciliation

A week after the diagnosis, my sisters were in Kent. Beta was cooking healthy, digestible meals for our father, and Suzanne had moved her hands in the air above him on his bed, some esoteric attempt at healing that, regardless of whether it could work, gave him a warm sense of her care. But my sisters were staying only a week, and we had to figure out a plan.

My father wanted his routine to stay as normal as possible. He wanted to do the radiation, but not the chemo: why suffer more in his limited time. The oncologist had said pain could be controlled but that the final stages "could be messy." He had warned us that our father also had a weak heart.

Who would take care of him over these months?

Charlotte, perhaps betraying her era, told me privately that an unmarried daughter—Suzanne—ought to move to Kent to take care of her father. I defended Suzanne's desire to stay out West, where, after our mother's death, she had entered the Ramtha School of Enlightenment in Washington state. Suzanne was on a spiritual quest, and ongoing events at Ramtha were important.

Beta and her husband Charles had become the parents of an adopted baby girl, Juliana. And both being full-time professors at UNLV, they had to remain in Nevada.

Only I could be in Kent regularly.

Fortunately, two trusted Kent people would help out. Ann volunteered to make dinners most nights and keep my father company after she got home from work. And Louise, a former social worker who already did odd jobs for my father, was happy to do more.

My father made his own decision. Feeling that Charlotte depended on me, he asked only that I stay with him two days each week. I wasn't far away, so of course I could go to Kent anytime. I began to notice in myself the seed of a whole new feeling: that my father needed my help.

* * *

I performed small tasks—shopping, cooking, driving my father to the bank or out for lunch. Meanwhile he quickly lost weight from the radiation. One particular appointment at the oncologist's stands out in my memory. My father sat on the examination table, his sunken chest bared. But here was the odd thing: I saw on my father's face the most elated smile I had ever seen—on him. He looked happy. "I've never felt so well taken care of," he told me, his son.

I came to see it this way: my father, a very private person, beneath his austere surface had always worried so much about his responsibilities and failures as husband, father, and artist that finally his illness gave him a chance to let go of some of that. He had a legitimate, fated reason now to feel he deserved care and love, himself.

And maybe, just maybe, I was forgiving him. I was helping him in practical ways that had never been needed before. I liked being the only one of his children there for him.

And I suspect that my father's having seen the warmth between me and Charlotte helped him trust me.

* * *

One evening out on the porch, my father said that I would be his estate's executor. Indulging in a rare drink of scotch, he was in a nostalgic good mood, talking about the past. He mentioned, with an amused little laugh, how, in his own psychoanalysis, he had realized only rather late that "my analyst didn't know the first damn thing about visual art!"

I said I agreed.

"But you know him much better than I do," he added.

Did I ever. I felt some anger filter into my mood. I reminded my father that it was he and my mother who had steered me toward the Doctor when I graduated from college. "Remember, you said he could become my *real friend*?"

He remembered.

I took a breath, and decided to do it: to divulge the secret. In a matter-of-fact tone, I said that the Doctor had "sexualized" the doctor-patient relationship with me. My father said nothing at first, so I said, "He seduced me." I hastily added, not wanting him to be confused, that I was not gay.

"He did that?"

I backtracked a little, because I also felt responsible. I had been an adult at the time, even if a naïve one, I said. I shouldn't have let it happen. It wasn't like I had been a twelve-year-old molested by a priest. On the other hand, it had taken me years to sort it all out and move on.

"He was unethical," my father said in a principled voice. "He should have stepped down as your analyst."

Stepped down? What an oddly formal way to put it. *Recused himself*, my father could have said—as though the Doctor had been capable of better judgment. Maybe my father was too surprised to sound more natural. But I did appreciate his earnest anger. I felt I'd removed a kind of hidden barrier between us. I would not have wanted him to die before we knew each other this much better.

* * *

I was in Charlotte's Manhattan kitchen when the phone rang. Louise told me she had found my father in his bed, that morning, dead of an apparent heart attack. In sleep his weak heart had saved him from cancer's messy ending. I was not detached: I sobbed immediately.

Louise added that she had found Blair the cat curled up beside my father's body on the bed. My father had long ago installed a screen door to his room, to let air circulate and to keep affectionate Blair out. On his last night, he had welcomed in his cat.

* * *

The service was held at the house. Stubborn late-winter snow lay in shadows under trees and bushes, defying the warm sunlight. A rabbit hopped toward the fence. I went back inside, where about forty people were sharing memories, and saw Charlotte standing, a martini in hand, between my sisters.

Charlotte hadn't spoken up during the formal sharing part of the service. Though a talker, she was surprisingly shy when talk was expected in front of a large group. But as I stepped to her, she whispered, not hiding her annoyance, "I heard your Uncle Howard claim he knew Nick longer than anyone else here. Not true."

My sole surviving uncle, Howard, was standing on the other side of the room—my mother's brother, who'd invented a valve and made lots of money. He noticed that I was looking at him, and he came over to us.

"Charlotte," he said, "I haven't had a chance to talk to you. It's wonderful that you were able make the trip."

"Why not?" she said. "It's wonderful that *you* could make the trip."

Howard smiled, not catching her drift. "We used to have the most perfect Thanksgivings in this house with Sally and Nick. You know, Charlotte, I knew Nick even before he married my little sister."

Charlotte stabbed her finger at him. "I knew Nicky when he was a baby... I attended his *father's wedding.*"

Howard's brow wrinkled, but he covered his doubt with a wink at me, as though Charlotte must be imagining things.

"It's true," I told him. "Charlotte was born in 1902, seventeen years before my father, and she saw my grandfather get married."

I was glad I stuck up for Charlotte's seniority at this gathering.

* * *

My sisters and I inherited equal shares of the Kent property. We agreed never to sell any part of the place that we loved. Since I lived in the area, I would supervise the upkeep of the property.

Like a revelation, I suddenly realized what Charlotte and I could do. Her Woodstock house had bad plumbing and dangerous little stairways and a rocky terrace. And it did not have almost a hundred acres of beautiful fields and woods. Instead of spending the warmer months in Woodstock, we could stay in Kent.

My sisters, both fond of Charlotte, had no objection.

So I offered Kent to Charlotte, and that's how we began the next chapter of our life together.

PART 3

22

Idyll of Kent

Inheritor, part owner, suddenly a man of property: that was me. I was finally in a position to give Charlotte possibilities equal to those she had already given me. We had all the beauty and space of a saltbox farmhouse on ninety-five acres of fields, woods, and streams in northwestern Connecticut. For five months of the year, there was no reason why our romance couldn't blossom forth in what had formerly been my parents' paradise. Or that's how I saw it.

Is anything as easy as it seems?

I had not known that a new furnace and reshingling of roofs were needed. More importantly, there were too many other people on or using the property. Ann still lived thirty feet away in my father's studio building. And Wendy, a friend of mine, had a long-established agreement with my father to use the barn and fields for her four or five horses. Hers was a regular small horse-riding business. She kept up the fences and barn in exchange for her riding students' coming for lessons. At any time, also, a man who shod the horses might appear. During our first summer in Kent, Charlotte and I felt as though Wendy were a co-owner of the property, because a student might walk by the porch as though we weren't there at all.

We had Charlotte's ancient Woodstock bed with its wooden pineapple posts brought to Kent so she would feel at home. Charlotte loved the farmhouse but insisted she have what she called her own private "apartment" in it. So I asked my carpenter neighbor Bill, who already harvested the hayfields, to divide my mother's large studio into two spaces. Charlotte's new digs had a skylight, extra closets, and a bathroom with her own deep soaking tub. We put a couch and chairs in her space so she could entertain guests. Because my small bedroom was just on the other side of the new wall and door, at night I could hear her call me about anything she needed.

But we could not forget how close Ann lived, just thirty feet away from Charlotte's bedroom window. As I lay in her bed one night, Charlotte shushed me, "Keep your voice down!" Ann might guess that we made love. Admittedly, there was also humor in this: we felt like two kids afraid of being found out.

I had not anticipated how great our need for privacy was.

Yet I hated the idea of asking Ann and Wendy to go. I was so shy and guilty about this that it took me until the following summer to ask them both to relocate. Thank God Ann found perfect lodgings on the other side of Kent. I softened the effect on Wendy by suggesting that Charlotte write a check to help her build a horse barn beside her own house. We—or rather Charlotte—gave Wendy and her husband Keith, also a friend of mine, twenty thousand dollars.

I had met and become friends with Keith and Wendy way back when I was of college age. Keith painted abstractions, but to make a living, he now worked as a night watchman at Kent School. It turned out that he enjoyed talking to Charlotte about art, literature, and her life. Keith often hired himself out as a driver, taking people to and from New York airports, so we hired him to transport us to and from the country each season.

In Manhattan I helped Charlotte pack her giant suitcase in an exacting order, a sequence that she insisted on. The process was so tedious that, to me, it felt like building a small temple in a box. In first went a foundation of a dozen pairs of shoes and sandals, each pair wrapped in tissue paper. Next in went underwear, what she called her "pants." Then layers, in order, of T-shirts, slips, socks, and stockings. Then bathrobes of different weights and colors, and slacks and jeans, and colorful shirts, immaculately folded so as not to wrinkle. Then skirts. Then dresses. Finally, on top, sweaters, jackets, and coats for any kind of weather. In the suitcase top's pocket, we must take high-quality wooden hangers. I had to sit on the suitcase to close it, and tie a rope around it lest it burst open. To be connected to an older woman with such amazing taste in exciting clothes was a joy of my life, but packing for her almost drove me crazy.

Keith picked us up in his Jeep Cherokee, and his calm, competent driving and jovial good company made the trip a pleasure. I passed around Charlotte's traditional hard-boiled eggs, each egg wrapped in wax paper. I might read a *New Yorker* story aloud. Keith would ask Charlotte questions about her experiences. On our first such move, when we neared Kent, Charlotte told us about a long walk she had taken fifty years earlier in the same area.

Charlotte's oldest friend was Josephine Tasman, who had lived on a Connecticut farm in the '30s. "Joe" would later drive buses and trucks around Manhattan while Charlotte worked in the Red Cross during World War II. But before that, when Charlotte visited Joe's farm and helped feed the pigs, the two women set off for a walk one morning. They walked and walked, at least twenty miles, until, as it got dark, they came across an establishment they had never heard of—Old Drover's Inn, in Dover Plains. "We had no money. Credit cards didn't exist," said Charlotte. "But the Inn took us in overnight and served us a fabulous meal *on trust. On our word.*" That was a different era.

* * *

From the start in Kent, Charlotte's presence somehow made the familiar family house new for me. Without her, the "ghosts" of my parents would have weighed too much on me. I was reminded of Wallace Stevens's lines in his *Notes Toward a Supreme Fiction*: "The poem refreshes life so that we share . . . the first idea . . . It satisfies/ Belief in an immaculate beginning." It was as if I could see the place anew, through Charlotte's eyes.

My best gift to Charlotte was a garden. I had cement and rocks of the barn's original foundation dug out so a remaining wall of stone built into the hill became a perfect backdrop for plants. My friend Paul, a gardener, orchestrated the flowers, herbs, and a few vegetables. Louise came up regularly to do weeding with me.

The scene felt somehow like a European style open-air café where we'd have our smoked salmon and martinis, far enough away from the house to ignore phone calls.

Of a late afternoon, Charlotte and I watched great spangled fritillaries and hummingbirds enjoy the flowers— zinnias, sunflowers, butterfly bushes, cones, marigolds.

But I could only wish our country life was that idyllic all the time. This would not be a truthful memoir if I did not admit my illusions of that time. I suppose I had imagined that we could have a perfect life. Maybe my ego, in defense of the huge age disparity, wanted to prove that our uniqueness could conquer all. Shouldn't my unmistakable, deep love for this woman solve all problems?

Our biggest problem was that, if I were out after dark, Charlotte was afraid. She felt dangerously isolated in an unfamiliar, rural house, whose fragile old glass windows would be child's play for someone to break into. There were no doormen guarding the premises, as in Manhattan. With trees in full leaf, no neighbors' lights could be seen. So Charlotte had a painful fear of a mysterious knock on the door, heightened by the fact that her eyesight wasn't what it used to be. Consequently, I felt duty-bound to never leave the house after dark.

I tried to be sympathetic, attributing Charlotte's fear only to her age. After all, crime was almost unheard of on the mountain; and I knew our neighbors, less than a quarter mile away, were good people.

Then Charlotte confessed to me, by way of a Woodstock story, that her fear was not new. When she was still quite young, in the 1950s, with Pat away in New York, Charlotte had been alone in her Woodstock house. There was a well-known, old-fashioned knife-grinder man who pushed his cart of knives and pots all around Woodstock. In the late afternoon, he happened to push his cart up Charlotte's driveway. Here is what Charlotte confessed, what perhaps she'd never told anyone before: way back then, she had become so afraid of the knife-grinder that she locked her door and cowered in a back room, pretending no one was home.

In Kent in the evenings, TV watching provided some good entertainment for Charlotte, but it could also cause trouble.

One evening, TV news reported an escaped convict loose in the Hartford area, about a hundred miles from us. With her plastic sense of geography and time, Charlotte reacted as though the convict could appear any minute at our door. It was similar to her fear that a Florida hurricane could reach us in an hour or two. She seemed to live in a space-time that made no sense. I was losing patience with her irrationality.

Charlotte told me, "Buy a gun!"

"I'm not a gun kind of person," I said.

She would escape by hiding in the silo, she said. (I'd added wooden stairs to make its high opening accessible.)

"That would be a cul-de-sac, not good," I said.

* * *

An incident later that same summer taught me the lesson that Charlotte's fears were not always unreasonable. One evening Keith called about a convict on the run. As night watchman at nearby Kent School, Keith was in the loop of local police activity. It was exquisitely ironic that he warned us that an armed and dangerous *escaped convict* was actually on the loose on our mountain.

"Lock your doors. Be careful," said Keith. The police had formed a perimeter to close in on the convict. We would learn later that the convict ditched his car and ran into the woods, and was apprehended about a mile from us.

Charlotte could say, *I told you that such things can happen anywhere.* If occasionally paranoid, Charlotte also had far more experience than I. I preferred donning the coat of the rational man, saying, "What are the chances?" But how much of life had I seen?

One reason Charlotte could imagine the disaster of home invasion was her memory of an event on July 24, 1946. Charlotte's close cousin Marjorie Church Logan and her daughter Jeanne lived in the fashionable Long Island town of Flower Hill, where such things were not supposed to happen. But in broad daylight, a burglar entered their Georgian mansion. Angry over getting only sixty dollars, he shot Marjorie dead with his .32-caliber nickel-plated Saturday night special. Then he raped Jean and shot her in the head. Amazingly, Jean crawled to a neighbor's house and survived, later to marry the tennis pro Stan Smith and raise a family.

"You don't know about murder until it happens to someone you love," said Charlotte.

She knew about being accused of murder, as well. When she and Pat had been out west on vacation, they saw newspaper headlines naming Pat as a murder suspect back in New York. His young female painting assistant had been found dead on the pavement below his high studio window. The artist, presumably, could have pushed her out. Pat and Charlotte went back to New York to confront the charge. The girl's diary, once found, sadly showed that the girl was mentally unstable, had fallen in love with Pat, and committed suicide.

* * *

Fortunately, by the end of our second summer, we developed a country routine whose regularity reduced Charlotte's fears. Louise, who had helped my father, cooked pies for us each week. She bathed Charlotte's feet in hot water to make trimming her tough toenails easier. And Louise volunteered to spend the occasional evening at the house so that I could do something at night.

Pauline, the mother of a grade school friend of mine, was a nearby neighbor. She and Charlotte hit it off, so I would drive Charlotte up to Pauline's house for drinks and storytelling.

And Josephine Tasman, Charlotte's companion on that long country walk fifty years earlier, now lived in nearby Sherman. Calm, quiet Joe enjoyed the excitement of Charlotte's bolder, social etiquette–defying style. We attended a few dinners at Joe's house, and Joe spent a night or two with Charlotte so I could go into Manhattan to pick up Charlotte's mail, since she didn't trust the postal service to forward it.

Charlotte probably told Joe about our intimacy. I knew this because of what Joe confided to me one day. She said that she liked me more than either of Charlotte's husbands. It was a huge compliment. (Years later, Joe would tell me, "You'll never find anyone like Charlotte again.")

Our life in Kent became less about potential traumas and more about small country adventures. One night I heard Charlotte scream, and I ran into her room. "An *animal* jumped on me!" She touched her chest. "Right here!" Had she dreamt it? Then we heard a rustling sound from her wastebasket, and a baby red squirrel climbed up its edge and looked at us. I used Charlotte's cane to herd the intruder out the breezeway door.

"Whew! Red squirrels are more aggressive than gray squirrels," said Charlotte.

Proof positive of Charlotte's feeling at home was her walking the environs, very much as she had around her Woodstock house. She would point with her cane and declare, "These lilacs need trimming before they block the front door." Or, "This fir must come down— other trees need the light." "These sticks need picking up, good kindling for the fall." Now the woman of the house, she took a proprietary interest. And since I was a proud owner of the property, I never felt like a butler or servant.

* * *

The highlight of the summer was our July 14 Bastille Day party. It was Charlotte's idea, but our guests were my friends, all my age. I had never forgotten Ed's reproach in Woodstock that I was "living too old," so I felt vindicated now in sticking to my guns: I could be with Charlotte and still socialize with my age group.

For the party I created a golf course on the lawn. I dug nine holes and stuck in empty cans from foods that Charlotte and I had eaten, so a ball dropping in would make a satisfying "clunk." Each hole had a tomato stake flagstick with a label: #1 Consommé Madrilène, #2 Chicken Soup, #3 Artichoke Hearts. With my computer I designed scorecards that had a photo of Charlotte and me in the garden.

Charlotte wanted to look her best for the party.

"Eyes," she said. So, with a moist Q-tip, I gently cleaned any morning gunk from around her eyes and lashes.

"Hearing aid," she said. I scraped earwax off the plastic so she could put it in her ear.

"I'm shedding like an old dog," she declared, which was my cue to pick loose white hairs off her blue suit with red scalloped fringes.

"Pins," she reminded me. I attached safety pins to keep her slip in place.

"Red badge of courage." That's what she called her Hot Coral Red lipstick, kept in her Venetian case with mirror. Her quote of the famous book's title was her way of admitting how nervous she was going into the social situation. With a practiced hand, pretending to use the mirror, she could apply her lipstick by touch.

I can still see, in memory, the sheer effort of her preparation: the concentration in her pale forehead, delicacy of bone at her temples, how her slender hips shook with the work to make her appearance right. Finally, on with her Venetian gondolier's hat, and she was ready.

She reminded me of a bullfighter getting dressed to perform in the ring. Maybe this was because, in fact, Hemingway in the '30s had escorted her and Bunny to a bullfight in Spain. So I imagined Charlotte resembling the bullfighter Romero in *The Sun Also Rises*, dressing for the challenge. It took some courage for a woman fifty years older than anyone else, and secretly my lover, to entertain our guests.

Our guests were three other couples: Keith and Wendy, Joel and Tonia, and Paul and Moira. I'd known Joel and Paul since the fourth grade. Choosing putters and colored golf balls, we played the course. Charlotte turned her cane upside-down to hit one golf shot with its handle, her ball scampering straight toward Consommé Madrilène. Then she and Wendy chose to relax with martinis in the garden.

High field weeds bordering the lawn captured many shots. Humor was the point, not competition. Using his putter like a scythe to find his ball, Joel struck a horseshoe. Paul ricocheted a shot off the silo. By the time we reached the last hole, next to the garden, in the shadow from the wooded hill above, a hovering monarch butterfly lit on Moira's red ball.

"He's attracted by the color, looking for a female," said Charlotte.

Moira sank her putt: our winner.

We had champagne, melon and prosciutto, roast beef, and ice cream with blueberries on the porch. In honor of Charlotte, I put on some Cole Porter, and she danced with Keith, as I danced with Tonia. Then, settling down, Charlotte told us why she always wanted to celebrate Bastille Day.

She had traveled to Spain during the Spanish Civil War, because Bunny was sent to interview Franco. After Bunny crossed enemy lines, Charlotte waited for his return in a Basque seaside town, Saint Jean-de-Luz. The town was mostly empty, but for strange characters and possibly spies. Two French destroyers were docked in the harbor. In the evenings, for days, Charlotte sat at an outdoor café waiting for a message from Bunny. Then suddenly one night, the sky lit up with frightening explosions, and Charlotte ducked under her table, afraid the fighting had spread. Her waiter smiled and informed her that it was Bastille Day: the ships were celebrating with fireworks. And he handed her a message: "Still alive. See you soon. Bunny."

"He was white as a sheet when he returned," Charlotte told us, "because he'd seen the bodies from the war piled on train cars."

23

Gone Fishing

With everything more shipshape in Kent, I no longer had any excuse not to take a trip by myself. After eight years of being with Charlotte, I wanted a vacation: a time to know who I was outside of her presence.

To fend off my usual travel anxiety, I reminded myself that earlier in my life I had traveled alone to many places, like Chicago, Colorado, Puerto Rico, Italy, Paris, and Greece. Traveling alone meant freedom, unencumbered by needing to please any companion. But where could I go now? I remembered my sister Beta lauding her trip with Charles to Montauk, a fishing town at the far end of Long Island. It would be a new destination, a manageable adventure.

The idea of *fishing*, in particular, appealed to me. Like most rural kids, I'd fished as a boy, often for catfish, and once in a stream, I caught a trout with my bare hands. My father had taken me fishing in a rowboat, his best-ever fatherly gift.

But fishing was also an artistic idea for me.

In free-association sketches I often drew a fisherman-as-artist casting his line into water. The act was symbolic: the artist dips his line into himself, into his own unconscious, to find an inspiration. He might hook a fish, or a shoe, a dead or a live body, a whale too big for his little boat, a dream or a nightmare. On paper or canvas, it's rather like life itself: we "fish" all the time, not knowing what will happen next.

While I was away, Joe stayed with Charlotte, and Louise and Keith were on call if needed.

I took a train into the city and a bus out to Long Island, where I rented a car. After checking into a seaside hotel, I drove to Montauk, where a sign caught my attention: "The *Lazy Bones*—Fishing Excursions." The boat went out for flounder in a saltwater lake by the ocean.

I was reminded of a mural above the bathtub in Kent that my mother had painted for us when we were little, a painting of lobsters and a flounder with both its eyes weirdly on the same side of its body. My sister Beta's first-ever memory was of a flounder.

On board the *Lazy Bones*, Captain Mike showed us how to bait our hooks with mussels. Each of our lines held two hooks.

"Flounder hibernate all winter," Captain Mike told us. "Flat in the mud, they take a long time to wake up, so the downside eye migrates to the side that's up."

I lowered my line and waited for a nibble. Within moments, everyone else was hooking flounder, including a boy of about eight, and the crew ran from person to person, taking fish off hooks, celebrating and taking photos. Still I felt no nibble.

My dark side asked: what's wrong with me, why are fish ignoring me?

Then my rod bent, and I reeled in two flounder at once, one on each hook. "Big winner here! Double-header here!" yelled Captain Mike. Apparently it was almost like a hole-in-one for a golfer. "I can't believe it," said the Captain. "A beginner gets the only double-header so far this season!" That night I found a restaurant specializing in cooking your own catch, and I dined on mine.

Back at my hotel, being of a symbolic temperament, I looked for meaning. Wasn't I a bit like a flounder, myself? Cautious, afraid of the world . . . like a flounder, I was slow to wake up—to leave the mud of childhood. And yet, if blind in some ways, I also had acute vision, like two eyes on one side.

If anyone had helped me survive the mud, to see better, it was Charlotte. I had needed time away to appreciate her.

The next morning, before I started home, I walked the white sand outside my hotel. Waves reflecting the sun scrolled in like molten silver. I remembered the dream I'd had that night. From the shore I watched a magnificent sailing ship, on which I could see my mother, the ship's captain, surrounded by her crew, made up of famous artists, writers, and thinkers. As I watched, the crew raised crossbows and fired sharp arrows toward me. But in mid-air, the arrows became paintbrushes with red-paint tips, and before landing at my feet, the brushes transformed into long-stemmed red roses. Danger had become beauty. From far away, I strained to see my mother's face. In sudden close-up, I saw her mouth open wide, like a fish in a medieval painting by Hieronymus Bosch. She tried to speak, but no words came.

I was back in Kent by nightfall. Charlotte proudly showed me how she and Joe had washed clean every greasy dish and pot I had ignored in the kitchen cabinets.

A day later I found a small strip of passport photos that my mother had once given to me, when I was perhaps twenty. She had taken the photos of herself not for travel, but to record how she'd actually felt at the time, when I was about a year old. She had been too proud, or ashamed, to let others see her desperation in a painful marriage. But her private photos showed the pain and depression etched in her face. Like her silent face in my dream, the pictures were a confession.

24

Poems and Paintings

At age ninety-three, during our fifth summer in Kent, Charlotte began writing poetry. My friend Harmon Smith had started a writers' group, so Charlotte joined us. I was writing short stories and had begun a novel based on my life with Charlotte. To make it easy for Charlotte, we always met at my house, about once a month.

Harmon, once my father's best friend, was the author of the book *My Friend, My Friend—The Story of Thoreau's Relationship with Emerson*. Tora Givotosky regularly published her poems in journals. Earl Brecher was a jack-of-all-trades, writer of stories, poetry, and memoir. We were a friendly group, but we could be tough on each other when necessary. Charlotte made genuine friends of these people.

Charlotte's poems, whether about a distant past or the present, were clear and direct. Here is one about her childhood:

Sleigh Ride

I peek out from under
the stiff buffalo cover,
and feel intense cold.
The whiteness
startles me with
its density.

> I can see the
> rump of the horse
> rising up and down
> and hear the jangling
> of the bells

Most of her poems were about the present:

> The tan silo stands erect
> against the cerulean sky.
> The stark, white robust birch
> follows and leans affectionately
> against its side.

And she displayed a sly humor:

> The big black cricket
> stands with knees
> way above his head.

* * *

Painting was still my major creative outlet.

My packing and unpacking of Charlotte's clothes touched off an entire series of pictures. It started with one humble object: a clothes hanger. My strength had always been line, and a wire hanger *is* a line. I drew and painted hangers, closets, and clothes. A typical closet— rod, hangers, shelf, light bulb—provided a framework to which I added the spontaneous color and near-abstraction of clothing. Then a woman could appear, often nude, picking out clothes to wear.

I invented Hangerman, a cartoonlike character whose body was made entirely of hangers. In a cartoon book, I told how Hangerman was "born" in a closet before venturing out to explore the world, where he eventually found his Hangerwoman. I also made a life-size, suspended sculpture of Hangerman. And finally, using my video drawing table, I produced a video art piece about Hangerman being interviewed on TV. Of course Hangerman was a side of myself: a vulnerable guy trying to find his place in the world.

I was offered a show in a new, informal country gallery, and I invited my friends Joel and Keith to show their work with me. Our opening came on a scorching, hot July day. Charlotte gallantly sweated her way through it. Only one of us, Joel, sold a piece. This time, as opposed to in Woodstock, I did not take my not selling to mean that my art was worthless.

25

My Affair

At a spring party in 1996 at Joel's house, Joel's younger sister Jenny sat next to me as we balanced plates of food on our laps. Charlotte was talking with Tonia on the other side of the room.

Jenny had always been pretty, with thick, dark hair, and as we talked, I discovered that we were flirting.

A few days later, Jenny phoned me. "I'm breaking my own dating rules," she said. "The man is supposed to call first, but to hell with that. You're invited for dinner."

Our two families had been close, so little of the get-acquainted process was necessary. As a kid I had slept over at Joel's, with Jenny across the hallway. Their mother, Phyllis, had been a good friend of both my parents. I knew the basics about Jenny. She was divorced. Her two young-adult sons no longer lived with her. She was a social worker who helped elderly or disabled people negotiate the system. And Jenny was no stranger to hardship—you wouldn't guess it, but she had MS, which could affect her in subtle and unpredictable ways.

I knew that my going to Jenny's would upset Charlotte. But I also knew that ignoring my impulse would make me resentful. I was still a young man. I wasn't about to try and sneak around behind Charlotte's back. I remembered that day in Woodstock after the party at Jan and Ed's, when Charlotte agreed I could see younger women and still come back to her.

So while we were sitting in the garden having our martinis, I told her about my date with Jenny. A ruby-throated hummingbird was hovering over flowers, and Blair the cat rolled on a catnip plant. I simply said that I would go to Jenny's for dinner. That was all I said: dinner.

"The garden is full of weeds," she said, as though not hearing me. "You have to get down on your hands and knees and weed. You and Louise have work to do."

"Did you hear me?" I asked.

"Yes, you want to have sex with Jenny."

Charlotte was not wrong. But hearing it said so bluntly made me feel guilty, which in turn made me angry. Draining my martini, I said, "When you were *my age*, you did a lot more than I'm doing . . . you had your affair with Aldo when you were *married* to Bunny, and then started with Pat when you knew Aldo!"

"Ha!" Charlotte said loudly. "You already had lots of girlfriends before you met me!"

I'd had my share, but Charlotte exaggerated.

We were at a standoff.

In a baleful, or satiric, tone—I couldn't tell—Charlotte slowly said, "Life is bare, full of misery everywhere"—from some poem or other she knew. Next, lighter-toned, she said, "Don't take it serious, it's too mysterious."

I was thinking, love doesn't solve everything. Of course I loved Charlotte—Jenny was no threat to that. I supposed that my anger came more from a need to feel I had a *right* to see Jenny. After all, living with Charlotte was in some ways insular. Hadn't I been good for a very long time, in spurning all other women? Unfortunately, such obsessive thoughts just fed my anger.

"*Your age* dominates everything," I said.

I couldn't believe I'd made such a cruel remark.

Tough Charlotte didn't seem to flinch. She coolly said, "When I'm gone, you can do *anything* you want."

But then she lifted her cane, and with a sweeping motion she tossed it deep into the garden.

Obstinate, silent, I refused to retrieve it for her.

So Charlotte raised the ante. She stood up and walked—too quickly, dangerously—into the garden. Terrified she'd fall, I yelled, *"Be careful!"*

She glared stubbornly back at me from behind the tall Mexican sunflowers.

She had won: I gave in. Wading into the flowers, I picked up her cane and extended my hand to her, so I could guide her safely back to her chair.

We both settled down. "You always go round and round," she wistfully told me. She had written a poem titled "Round and Round" about the changing seasons. Even if my own moodiness confused me, she seemed to be saying, my moods were as predictable to her as the seasons.

"Just go on your date," she said with acceptance.

We carefully organized Charlotte's bedroom before I left for Jenny's. In close reach on her bedside table were a glass of water, her sleeping pill in a cup, five lemon cough drops, and the phone, with a sheet of important numbers printed extra large. The path to the bathroom was free and clear.

Having had an early dinner, she told me not to worry, that she would simply go to sleep early. She clutched my hand. "Please watch out for cars backing out of driveways. Wake me when you get back." Charlotte laughed. "You'd think you were going to the moon! I love you."

"I love *you*," I said.

Her generosity, after the explosion in the garden, was astounding to me.

I drove the forty minutes to Jenny's. Her cottage was perched on a sharply rising lawn. To reach her front door, I skirted around a five-foot-high stone retainer wall in the lawn's center, where a small birch tree grew.

Jenny had roasted two game hens. As we ate, she asked me if I remembered kissing her when I was about fifteen and she twelve, when we'd played checkers at my house. I did, but back then she had been only a friend's little sister.

"Kind sir," she said, "I just want to get something straight. You are a single gentleman, not seeing anyone else—correct? I mean, I have no idea what you do when you're in New York."

I took a moment to answer.

"I'm not dating anyone, if that's what you mean."

"Good," she said.

I made a decision that I hoped not to regret.

"You're going to think this strange . . . ," I began.

"Okay, spit it out," she said.

"I don't just *take care* of Charlotte. What I mean is . . . it's a complete relationship—between me and her. Intimate."

Jenny looked confused.

I backpedaled. "I'm a normal guy." It was difficult to tell. "She's been my lover, and I know that sounds strange. She understands about me and younger women."

"Peter, you weird bastard. You're so damned full of surprises."

"Hardly anyone knows about it," I said.

"That would make sense," she said dryly.

"I guess I sure blew it with you tonight, didn't I?" I said, thinking I'd eliminated any chance for romance.

"Just give me a moment." She went to open another bottle of wine before we both moved to the couch. "Look, Peter, I'm an open-minded person. I've known some amazing older people in my work."

I was skeptical that she'd ever met anyone like Charlotte, but apparently Jenny didn't see me as some kind of monster. Even if nothing happened with this sexy woman, I was glad I'd told the truth.

"I like your honesty," she said. "You're a middle-aged man with a bunch of baggage, but you do have your good points."

She moved closer, we kissed, and she was a great kisser. With wine in tow, she invited me upstairs. In bed, we both smoked. She had beautiful wide hips. We had sex.

When I left, she said, "Don't be a stranger, Peter."

Having had a lot to drink, walking in the dark down her steep lawn,

I forgot about the stonewall drop-off. My left foot stepped into thin air, and I would have fallen, but luckily my right hand was touching the birch tree growing from the base of the wall, balancing me. With one long, descending step, I landed safely five feet down and just kept walking.

Back at my house, I woke Charlotte, as she had asked me to. "I'm glad you're back," she said.

I would see Jenny several more times over the summer. Charlotte never complained. My affair with Jenny ended when Charlotte and I moved back to Manhattan.

* * *

As it turned out, our golden age in Kent survived even my affair. Charlotte and I enjoyed our best times as she grew from being old toward "ancient," from 1993 to 1997. Our bedroom life continued. Maybe Charlotte expressed it best after we took a particularly fine walk outside the farmhouse on a moonlit night. She stopped to stroke Blair the cat's glowing white belly with the soft rubber tip of her cane. After our walk, as we lay in bed together, she said, "Someday we'll remember these as the good old days." She was ninety-four.

PART 4

26

A Fall at the Opera

Our matinee afternoon at Lincoln Center started out fine, with Wynne joining us for lunch at the Metropolitan Opera before we saw *La Bohème*. As we ate, Charlotte spilled her red wine, so Wynne, an immaculate diner, sopped it up with a napkin. Then, like a tradition between them, and because the opera was about poor artists, the two old friends again debated the value of Hemingway.

"He had to bop a pigeon just to be able to eat in Paris, to not starve, as a young man," Charlotte said.

"Dear Charlotte, that is irrelevant. He was a male chauvinist of the first order."

"He couldn't have been *nicer* when I met him," countered Charlotte. "He saved me when I ate glass!"

Wynne gave me a nod, knowing Charlotte *would* tell her favorite story about the writer. It happened in the '30s, when writer Bunny and Charlotte were invited to a country dinner in Spain. Charlotte sat next to Hemingway. "I was eating anchovies and greens out of an old glass jar," Charlotte told us, "when I chomped on something hard—glass."

Afraid she'd swallowed tiny shards of glass, she asked Hemingway what to do. Eat the soft insides of the rolls, he said, and you'll be fine. Thus introduced, when dinner ended, Hemingway proposed taking her outside to show her what a real Spanish town was. He took her hand, and they walked through the streets and talked, at last reaching a fabulous, romantic view of the town. Here, in her story, Charlotte paused for effect. As they enjoyed the perfect view, from a window above them a *pot de chamber* was emptied, its contents splashing at their feet.

"A charming story, dear Charlotte," said Wynne, "but he was a chauvinist."

"War shrapnel came out of his body his whole life. That would drive anyone mad!"

It was time for the opera. Our mezzanine seats were excellent. I wasn't a fan of opera, but I did like *La Bohème*. At the first intermission, I got up to go to the men's room. "I have penis envy," Charlotte told Wynne. "The line to the women's is much longer than to the men's."

When I returned, I heard shouts, and several people were rushing to an area of seats a few rows from us. A seat's back was crumpled down. Charlotte turned her head from side to side, frustrated, trying to see what was going on. She murmured, "I can't see."

Word of mouth told us that a man had fallen, or jumped, from a high balcony. Since it happened during intermission, no one else was injured. Charlotte told me that she had only vaguely glimpsed, out of the corner of her eye, a falling shape—she'd thought it was someone's coat.

The rest of the opera was canceled.

After sharing a taxi to the East Side with Wynne, Charlotte and I watched TV news about the tragic suicide at Lincoln Center: a life-long opera lover, dying of cancer, had waited until intermission to leap to his death.

But that drama wasn't uppermost in my mind. Rather, now I was aware of what Charlotte had been hiding, and perhaps hadn't wanted to admit to herself: she was losing her eyesight.

Within a few days, we went to Charlotte's optometrist, Dr. Cole, a woman of about eighty. The doctor had apparently known the condition was slowly developing over time. She said that Charlotte's macular degeneracy was the more serious, "wet" kind. The center of vision was already nearly gone. "Charlotte, honey, you'll never go *completely* blind," Dr. Cole told her.

Better peripheral vision had allowed Charlotte to manage until now. At least she could still walk around, maneuver in the world. But once-voracious reader Charlotte struggled to read at all. And socializing Charlotte could not see the expression on anyone's face. Various vitamins for the eyes and ocular devices were recommended.

But at ninety-five, Charlotte refused to take ocular vitamins that she called "big enough to choke a horse." And she did not have the patience to fuss with the knobs of a video magnifying reading machine. Personally, I admired her refusal to follow other people's well-meaning directions; she said screw it, I'll adjust in my own way.

Fortunately, Charlotte liked being read to, and we could afford to hire readers. And as always, she could make a real friend of someone working for her. Through an acquaintance, we found Amanda, a woman of about fifty living two blocks away. A cultured person, Amanda imported handmade art and cards, mostly from Africa. She enjoyed reading, and even more, the exciting conversations she could have with Charlotte.

* * *

One snowy city evening of that winter stands out in my memory. Despite sleet and snow, Charlotte flatly refused to allow me to walk her the three blocks to meet Wynne for dinner at The Beach Café. Cane in hand, bulked up in her bright red coat, she went out alone. In the apartment I waited, feeling powerless, wondering if she could safely traverse the slippery pavement to dinner and back.

It was excruciating. I thought, *This must be the price of love.* I almost went out, my plan being to hide from view outside the restaurant so I could intercept her coming out, even if she resented my doing it. But I weighed my own fear for her against how important Charlotte's sense of her independence was to her. I concluded that I should respect her confidence in herself, so vital to her enjoyment of life.

Finally, a loud *bang*—Charlotte throwing her cane into the umbrella stand outside her apartment door. She loved to do that. I opened the door. She looked utterly exhausted, her coat wet with melting snow, as she stepped close and nestled her face in my chest. She exhaled a sigh of relief. She had made it home.

27

Goodbye to the Doctor

If Charlotte tenaciously hung onto the pleasures of life, the same wasn't true for that other, once-dominant figure in my life, the Doctor.

He had phoned me from Gracie Mansion Hospital, a drug and alcohol rehab center on the Upper East Side. Joking, he said he was there for the free meals and board, since his insurance paid the bill. But his alcoholism was no joke. He told me that all the other patients respectfully called him "Doctor," but that a guard had bluntly criticized him, "You'll never learn, because you think you're better than other people." The Doctor's own patients thought he was away on vacation, but he wanted someone—me—to know where he actually was.

Now, a few months later, a New York detective phoned me. A doorman had discovered the Doctor dead on the floor of his apartment. The detective had found my phone number on the desk.

With no witnesses as to what had happened, the apartment was considered a crime scene. Until a coroner's report verified no "foul play," the door was closed off with yellow police tape. The detective had found no family phone numbers, bank records, or even a Social Security number— only my phone number. Barring more information, the city would bury the body in Potter's Field and auction off the apartment's contents.

I told the detective that the Doctor had once intended to make me his executor, or so he'd told me; but whether he had done it, I didn't know. The detective asked, could I come down right away? Maybe I could find something the police had missed, like a key to a safety deposit box that might contain a will.

Charlotte, for moral support, asked, "Do you want me to go with you?" No, I'd be all right.

The detective, unable to be there, had said I could pull away the yellow tape to enter. The body had already been taken to the coroner's. As I entered, I smelled a slight, unpleasant odor, which the detective had warned me about.

It was a sad, forlorn scene. The desk and couch hadn't moved an inch for decades. As ever, not a single painting was on a wall, only hundreds of books on shelves. In the little kitchen, there wasn't a scrap of food—he'd always gone out to eat.

I felt some guilty excitement. How many former patients get to explore their analyst's private space? The police had emptied the desk drawers on top of the desk, creating a pyramid of messy papers: photocopied articles, notepads, envelopes. I found a shopping list: "milk, scotch, tissues, cigarettes."

Under the paper were those talismanic gifts to the Doctor from patients who'd "graduated" from analysis: a sand dollar, a white pipe, a plastic swimmer, a coiled little brass salamander. The salamander felt familiar in my hand, a tactile memory from my childhood. I realized that my mother must have given it to him, so I put it in my pocket.

I checked behind some books, any likely place. But I found no key, no bankbook, and no evidence that I was executor. I tried to think. One idea occurred to me. Using the Doctor's phone, I dialed Gracie Square Hospital, where he'd tried to dry out. A woman there explained that they could not provide his Social Security number unless they received an official letter from the city morgue.

I hung up. At least I could give the detective a lead.

The phone rang. From the answering machine came the Doctor's voice. "I am not available at the moment, but kindly leave your name and message, and I will get back to you."

I picked up, and told the detective about Gracie Square. He thanked me but said that since I had not found anything, I must leave. I asked if I could arrange for a funeral home to receive the body, and take care of a burial. That was fine—I would save the city some money.

I sat silently on the couch before leaving. I felt no grief for the Doctor. Hadn't I cared for him? Certainly he had loved me—he'd once told me, "Peter, you have a beautiful soul." Then I realized that I had already grieved for the best of the Doctor, because he had been gradually dying for years.

I had forgotten something—the portrait of the Doctor by Bradley Phillips, which years ago the Doctor had intended to will to me. I went to the clothes closet, and there, behind his hanging suits, was the wooden crate. Even though nervous that a doorman might be suspicious, I carried the crate out and left the building—for the last time.

* * *

A few days later, to my surprise, I got a call from another former patient of the Doctor. I'd never heard of him. I shared the coroner's report: the Doctor's heart had given out, related to cirrhosis of the liver. This person, who seemed to know less about his analyst's private struggles than I, was arranging a small service for the Doctor. He had rented a hotel space for it.

About six people attended. I did not make remarks, though I did bring the portrait as a centerpiece to go with flowers. The organizer had located a distant cousin who would have the cremains put in a cemetery.

As people left the service, a middle-aged woman spoke to me. Her father had been a famous scholar. Decades ago, she said, her family had worried about the young man named John who went to study in Europe. "John needed guidance," she told me. "He was more of a philosopher, not an analyst. He wasn't a healer."

28

Time's Losses

In Kent, Charlotte and I took our favorite walk along a path that I'd had mown through the near hay field. On the barn at the path's start I had hung a double-sided sign reading *Charlotte's Way* on one side, with a color sketch of Charlotte's Venetian hat and a gondola on the other.

This afternoon, we sat in plastic chairs at the far end of the field, spikey cut hay at our feet. I brought smoked salmon and lemonade, to stay a while. Charlotte wore her denim jacket, blue jeans, short white socks and beaded moccasins. She pointed at a looming shape against the sky, and warned me that a giant vine must be choking that tree. And she saw the motion of a fluttering butterfly, which happened to be her favorite, an orange-and-black great spangled fritillary. I went and picked some fluffy purple jimson flowers for her, from the gully of the old mud pond, and down there I tripped over some wild, green-turning-orange pumpkins.

It was at bedtime, about two weeks after that field walk, that I noticed a pinkish area on Charlotte's thigh. She insisted it was only from crossing her legs when she sat, but I should have been smarter. A few days later she complained of a stiff neck. A day later, she felt suddenly weak, and luckily I caught her before she keeled over.

I called my own doctor, Bradley, who generously visited us on a Saturday, took a blood sample, and had Sharon Hospital test it on Sunday. At ninety-five, Charlotte had Lyme disease. Why hadn't we used the DEET spray? Like many people, we had not taken Lyme seriously enough, until it happened. I figured that, probably, a tiny tick had climbed up past her short white sock to her bare leg when we were in the hay field.

The cure seemed worse for Charlotte than the disease. The side-effect of constipation, from the antibiotic, distended her stomach into a taut, round ball. She looked weirdly, anciently pregnant. But her arms and legs were thin, her appetite not good enough. Despite visiting health-care help, Charlotte asked me to give her enemas, which were only slightly effective. We struggled with the disease for two months. I became obsessed with keeping track of Charlotte's symptoms and trying to make sure her pill regimen was right. Finally, when nausea and constipation hit at the same time, I drove Charlotte to the nearby Sharon Hospital emergency room. They put her in intensive care.

Charlotte's reduced appetite seemed the worst problem. Her young male doctor, as we sat near Charlotte in bed, whispered to me, "It happens to the aged. You watch, I'll use a little psychology on her."

He said, "Charlotte. Charlotte! Can you hear me?"

"Of course I can," she answered, bleary-eyed.

"Charlotte, you're not eating enough because you're trying to kill yourself."

"I am *not* trying to kill myself!" she said. "I'd eat more if I could."

The doctor was skeptical, and looked insulted. So I angrily told him, "You have *no idea* who you're talking to. Who she really is."

"We'll see," said the all-knowing doctor.

After he left us, Charlotte shut her eyes and quoted Aldous Huxley: "Time must have a stop." She was very discouraged.

But the next morning, her doctor took me aside and sheepishly admitted, in not so many words, that a prescription error was causing Charlotte's poor appetite. "Blood work shows her Lanoxin dose, for her heart, is too high for her current weight, affecting her appetite." Those were the little yellow pills for fast heartbeat that she had taken ever since her hip broke.

The doctor cut her dose in half. Her appetite increased immediately.

And a test confirmed that Lyme disease was no longer active in her system.

When we got home, to my relief, my sister Beta called to say she could take a few days off from teaching in Nevada to come stay with Charlotte. I needed a break, now that the crisis was over. I'll never forget Beta's generosity. I took a short driving trip to Vermont. When I returned, Beta said she and Charlotte had had a wonderful time together.

* * *

By the time Charlotte turned ninety-six, our life had inevitably become more insular and routine. Maybe that is why my memory of that time has a blurred sameness to it, with fewer distinct incidents standing out. Though her mind was strong and her feelings intense, Charlotte was weaker. Despite her recovery, Lyme had taken a toll. Our world was bound to shrink.

During the Christmas season of 1998, for her ninety-seventh birthday on December 18, Charlotte dressed in her magenta wool suit with a toreador black-stitched jacket. We went out for a walk. Warm for the season, the day was sunny, our shadows linked on the sidewalk. Charlotte could still mimic a spirited stride, if not actual speed. We crossed 68th Street to the small park connected to Julia Richmond High School and sat down on the nearest bench. About forty yards away, children were climbing over a new, elaborate jungle gym, and one child rode a small concrete tortoise. Charlotte lit up a Camel, and blew smoke with satisfaction. "Ah, that's good."

That's when a tall, blonde woman in white pants came from near the children to stand looking down at us.

"There's no smoking here!" she said. "Didn't you see the sign?"

"No," Charlotte said. "I *can't see* the sign."

I hadn't even noticed the sign.

"It's the law," said the woman. "No smoking."

"Arrest me!" said Charlotte. "I'll smoke if I want to—get the police and arrest me!"

The woman scowled at me, as though I were responsible, and stalked away. I yelled after her, "The wind's blowing *our* way—not toward the children!"

Charlotte kept smoking. *"Fuck her, this cigarette is good."*

I couldn't contain my annoyance, so I got up and walked the forty yards to the woman. "My friend over there is ninety-six, and she's lived across the street since 1926, and she survived Lyme disease. She's only enjoying one lousy cigarette."

The woman glared at me. "Smoking is *stupid*. I know, I did it for twenty years."

"Charlotte's smarter than you, she doesn't inhale," I said.

The woman paused before she said, "You are a horrible man."

So then this horrible man and Charlotte walked to Second Avenue, and one block south, and enjoyed soup and salad at a good Italian café.

* * *

For Christmas, later that week, I put up a tree in the living room. Charlotte loved the smell of a fresh fir. Charlotte and Bunny had once used real, lit candles on their tree—until their spruce caught fire, and since Bunny was drunk, Charlotte had had to put out the fire.

As I often did on Christmas Eve, I made a few tree ornaments. For one, I drew a naked lady, trimmed her from the paper, and put her in a real lobster's tail shell, creating a Christmas mermaid. After dinner, at bedtime, we followed Charlotte's usual reading tradition. In bed beside her, I read aloud "The Night before Christmas," from a 1931 edition illustrated by Arthur Rackham, in which Santa is impish and crafty rather than fat and jolly. Next, as always, I read Beatrix Potter's *The Tailor of Gloucester*, wherein the mice, in the nick of time, secretly stitch a waistcoat for the sick old tailor.

* * *

When Easter came around, I stood on the tiny balcony of my studio on 74th Street, at sundown. Across the street below was an old

Greek Orthodox church with a beautifully weathered, gold-leafed dome, and as the street darkened, I watched Easter celebrants emerge from the church holding their lit candles—a river of stars. It was a quiet, ethereal moment, a respite from worrying about Charlotte's health.

But I wasn't only painting or writing in my studio. In a way that I thought was harmless, I was cheating on Charlotte. I had discovered the Internet, and I was drawn to the chat rooms of America Online. With Charlotte more frail, I suppose I needed a sexual outlet, and women online provided that. But I did not want to actually meet any of them.

Most attractive was an intelligent, well-read married woman from a dirt-poor coal miner's family, who told me about her intellectual discussions with a scholarly monk at a monastery near her home. At first we exchanged playfully flirtatious letters imitating all kinds of writing forms—a troubadour poem, a romance novel scene, an Eastern poem about a samurai and a maiden. After she sent photos of herself in the nude—she was slender, dark-haired, seductive—things got more serious. She wanted to meet me in Maine (I'd told her I had access to a house there). She said she could make a "deal" with her husband: if she agreed to have a "threesome" with him and another woman, he would let her meet me in Maine. I didn't say yes. But a week later, she wrote that she had already fulfilled her husband's request. I wasn't sure why, but I found her deal with her husband shocking. I would not go to Maine. She said I was an upper-class snob; and that was that.

At least my flirtation hadn't affected Charlotte.

* * *

After Charlotte turned ninety-seven in December 1998, I turned fifty the following May. Our birthday months were curiously appropriate to our larger "May-December" romance. More seriously, in my mind Charlotte really did represent the entire twentieth century, while I knew only its second half.

If I ever felt older than my years, it was because of my association with Charlotte. But mostly I felt very young by virtue of the extreme contrast of our ages. I focused on her age, not my own. I had no sense of approaching any kind of "mid-life crisis." Well, there would always be time for that later.

This I felt strongly: if I could help Charlotte reach an age *older than her parents had lived*, I would have done a good job. Or at least that might prove I was doing her no harm. Charlotte's mother had lived to ninety-three, her father to ninety-eight.

But I needed help. I could not do the job alone.

In New York, Maureen, the middle-aged Irish woman who had cleaned Charlotte's apartment for years, was our most important ally. She loved Charlotte, and she steadily took on a bigger role, staying on many extra daytime hours, making chicken soup, helping Charlotte dress, and taking her out shopping. And there was Amanda. For my birthday Charlotte had Amanda go out with her to carry back my gift, a large, handmade electric clock with little figures appearing to turn the wheels of time. As well as reading to Charlotte several times a week, Amanda helped me put Charlotte's poems between covers as a book we had bound at Kinko's. Charlotte titled it *Round and Round—Poems by Charlotte C. Collins,* and she chose a bright red cover.

When we went to the country, it was Keith who read to Charlotte three days a week. Louise weeded our garden, made pies, and cut Charlotte's toenails. Having once run a community for the elderly, Louise always had good advice.

In Kent the greatest threat to Charlotte's health was August heat. Just as for her mother, Charlotte told me, summer heat was her Achilles heel. And yet she stubbornly refused to leave her "apartment" to sleep in the part of the house made cooler by the stone basement and shade of the big maples. Her bedroom's skylight let in too much hot sunlight, and yet she refused air conditioning. I devised a secret plan to install an air conditioner anyway, hidden above the new wall of her space, but I never mustered the resolve to actually do it, to defy Charlotte.

Fortunately my neighbor Bill, who had built Charlotte's space, put a thick tarp over Charlotte's skylight to keep the sun out. He also installed a ceiling fan to circulate the air. Charlotte said that the fan looked like a giant spider on her ceiling, but she accepted it.

So we got through another summer intact.

Charlotte and I avoided talking much about the future, lest we invite time's inevitable disasters.

* * *

It was February in the city, and Charlotte was ninety-eight. One night, as I carefully moved closer to her, the metal springs of her bed creaked. "You're getting bigger around the middle," she said. "But don't worry, I love you the way you are."

I turned off her bedside lamp, and put my left arm around her. It was affectionate touch, but one that often led to sex of some kind. But on this night Charlotte caressed my hand and said with doubt in her voice, "I hope I can." Her body tightened, and then she sighed. "Sorry. I can't do it."

Looking back now, I wonder if Charlotte felt it her duty to please her man sexually. Perhaps that attitude was more prevalent for a woman born in 1902, of an earlier era. On the other hand, as far as I knew, she had always enjoyed our sex.

Here is an amazing fact. In all our years together, during which I had wanted sex on most nights, not once before now had she ever said no.

But finally it was over. She was done. I gently hugged her to show that I understood.

"I could scratch your back," she offered. "I know you like that."

"It's all right. You're tired."

She breathed out. "Ah, peace," she said.

And it really was okay, because we still had the comfort and warmth of touch and the closeness that was most important.

* * *

I am reminded of two of Charlotte's poems that reflected her growing sense of resignation.

Darkness

The darkness
passes over my eyelids
and I am not afraid.
It is strangely soothing.
The long-gone scent of heliotrope
and the sight of a luna moth
either by day or by night,
will never be forgotten

The Bed

I come home—
the bed is there
ready and waiting.
It never disappoints me,
sometimes the springs
complain—but really
not too much.
I lie down flat, and
either worry and stay awake
or fall asleep almost
immediately.
It is most reliable.
What of the
homeless?

* * *

Round and round: another season, and Charlotte was ninety-nine. As we walked home with our lawyer friend Eric from dinner out at Shabu-Shabu, Charlotte's shoe caught in a sidewalk crack and she went down. Eric and I half-carried, half-guided her to a pizza parlor where she could sit while Eric called for an ambulance. Holding her hand, I saw a trickle of blood creep down her wrist.

At the hospital the doctor pushed on Charlotte's upper arm, and with an audible snap, the bone settled back into her shoulder socket. Worse, X-rays revealed a hairline fracture of her pelvis. There was nothing to be done for that but let it slowly heal with time. We were home by midnight.

Charlotte told me she could "walk through the pain" of her pelvis so it would get better. She proudly demonstrated how, to reach her bathroom at night, she could stutter-step first to the radiator, for support, then to the filing cabinet, then to the bathroom doorknob. But one night I heard a thud, and I found Charlotte on the floor. She wasn't injured. But something had to change.

After a home consultation with Charlotte's new doctor (we called her "Dr. Wendy"), I reluctantly bought L-shaped metal contraptions to fit under and around Charlotte's mattress. They were restraining bars. I was overwhelmed by sadness over having to cage Charlotte in her own bed. In Maine a decade before, I had made the "Charlotte catcher" above the stairwell, which wasn't necessary. Now I had no choice. Now Charlotte wore a call-button around her neck, and I wore a receiver, so she could buzz me for help.

I also bought a wheelchair.

But we still had some good times. Frank came over for a dinner that we ordered take-out from L'Absinthe, our favorite French bistro. Our lobster, Dover sole, oysters, and baby lamb chops were the best take-out meal that Frank and I ever experienced. By this time, Frank had adopted Charlotte as his ideal of how vital and youthful an elderly person could be. He often dreamt about her. As he said good night to me by the elevator, his eyes filled with tears from seeing Charlotte in a wheelchair.

I should mention that Charlotte was not a person who felt sorry for herself, or expected anyone to feel sorry for her. She often seemed as determined as ever to enjoy life.

On the first warm, sunny day of spring, I took Charlotte out in her wheelchair to roll two blocks north to a pleasant space in front of the

Lenox Hill Neighborhood Association. For decades Charlotte had given Christmas checks to the association, because they housed and helped the elderly. Now she sat in her wheelchair near benches where other older people rested. Charlotte enjoyed a Camel before we pushed on to a favorite haunt of hers, The Beach Café. She greeted a friend who was also there for lunch. We didn't know that this would be Charlotte's last meal out at any restaurant.

* * *

A week later, I picked up the ringing kitchen phone. It was Jan, nephew Scotty's girlfriend in Virginia. She asked if I was sitting down. Then she said that Scotty had walked into the woods and shot himself.

In a most civilized way, Scotty had first called the local sheriff (a friend, who tried to argue him out of it), to say where his body would be found. He shot himself expertly, so to lessen the amount of blood. According to Jan, Scotty had been mired in a seasonal winter depression, made worse when he took a stand against local drug dealers. He became "paranoid" that the dealers were out to get him. Good citizen Scotty.

When I broke the news to Charlotte, she wept. Only twice before had I ever seen her sob openly. Once was for Wynne, after her son had put her in a nursing home in Washington state. Wynne had called Charlotte to say goodbye just before she died. The other time was for Judy, her other best and oldest friend from childhood. We had visited Judy in New Jersey shortly before she died.

Dr. Wendy, on her next visit, cautioned me about Charlotte's weight. She should eat more. Hearing this, Charlotte sat up in bed and loudly proclaimed, "Peter has become a very good cook!" Then, exhausted by defending me, she slumped back in bed.

In the living room, privately, Dr. Wendy gave me her opinion that Charlotte's wasn't eating enough because she was depressed over Scotty's suicide.

Charlotte depressed?

Depression happened to other people—not Charlotte. Or so I'd thought. I didn't want to believe it.

29

Temptation

Looking back, I want some excuse. I tell myself that I must have been anxious, sad, and bewildered by Charlotte's going downhill. I must have needed some outlet for built-up tension. But I don't know, for a fact, how much that explains it.

After online escapades that did not mean a thing, I finally met a woman who reached through the ether that had kept things safe.

Imelda worked part-time as a doctor's receptionist in Manhattan. What first got my attention was her standing only four feet, seven inches tall, so incredibly petite. And yet in her emailed photo she was voluptuous, with big breasts, olive skin, and luxuriant black hair down to her slender waist. She was forty-six, Puerto Rican, and divorced. She was living with her mother in a dangerous section of the Bronx until she could find her own apartment. She wrote that when shots rang out, she'd jump into the bathtub. She had grown up poor, her father running a small bodega, and after high school had gone to work. Imelda was so outside my experience, my world, that she seemed the most exotic creature I'd ever encountered.

In our second phone talk, I told Imelda about my real relationship with Charlotte. Rather than sounding shocked or judgmental, she seemed to respect me for it. It occurred to me that her cultural background dictated a special esteem for old people.

Since Maureen often stayed the afternoon with Charlotte, I invited

Imelda for a late lunch at Petaluma restaurant, near my studio. I watched Imelda get out of her cab: she wore a low-cut black blouse and a multi-colored skirt slit up to her hip. Standing next to her, for the first time in my life I felt like a very tall man. "Kind sir," she said, "I am here for you."

In Petaluma, Imelda ordered a pizza, and when the waiter brought it, she scolded him, "I ordered a *white* pizza!" and sent it back. I thought, this woman is as willfully confident as Charlotte.

And yet, at first, she also talked to me, bizarrely, as though she were at a job interview. I listened to her tick off her good points. She was about to study medical billing in a city-funded program, so she could get a better job. (The cost of the required textbooks was difficult for a poor person, she added.) Then she informed me that she could get along with all kinds of different people, fit in anywhere. She batted her eyelashes, saying, "See, I'm like an actress, baby. I got talent. I can make my eyes bold, like this, or charming, or sexy and alluding."

"All*ur*ing," I corrected her.

She nodded. "I make mistakes because I didn't get a big education like you. But I learn fast. On the reading comprehension for medical billing, I tested higher than anyone *ever* recorded." She laughed.

I was getting only the first installment of how weirdly smart this woman was. After our lunch, I invited her to my apartment.

On my couch, she assumed a formal, straight-backed pose, sitting far away from me, before rising to look at my paintings. "I see you have some skills," she said. Still on the couch, I looked up and she was suddenly close, looking down at me and wiggling her hips. "You like what you see, don't you? I saw you checking out my ass. But now I must go home to cook for my mother, even though we have little to eat."

I felt sympathy for her, since she'd had all kinds of hard knocks in her life that I could only imagine.

On impulse, before seeing her out, I offered to pay for her medical billing textbooks. I handed her a hundred and forty dollars, and some more cash for her taxi home. As we said goodbye out in the street, I leaned close for a little kiss, but she said, "I never kiss on a first date."

Back at Charlotte's, Maureen was waiting.

"Sorry I'm late," I said, putting down the groceries I'd bought.

"No bother. Charlotte said not to call you because you're working on your art."

Maureen handed me the clip-on receiver for the buzzer unit that Charlotte wore. As she put on her coat, Maureen filled me in. "Charlotte ate her oatmeal. Amanda read to her, very nice. I got Charlotte into her wheelchair, out to the living room, and trimmed her toenails. She's napping now."

"Good."

"See you tomorrow, then," she said, and left.

Thank God for Maureen. I peeked in on Charlotte, who was safely asleep behind those terrible bars I'd put in.

For dinner I planned to make baked potato and creamed spinach, easy for Charlotte to eat, and a small T-bone steak.

Before cooking, I paused by the open door of the maid's room just off the kitchen. We used it for storage. A huge cardboard box still held Alpine brand self-heating meals that Charlotte had insisted we buy before the millennium computer bug scare of the year 2000. She had remembered how the Red Cross stocked self-heating cans of food during World War II. Leaning against the wall was a framed poster, a painting of handsome Coast Guard seaman Pat at the wheel of a ship, with the words, "Setting the course for VICTORY." The image of wartime reminded me of when the Twin Towers fell. We had been safely away in Connecticut, but after I heard the news on my car radio, I was afraid that Charlotte might freak out when I told her. But she calmly said, "Just like World War II. What do people expect in this world?"

I pulled myself out of memory and made dinner. Later, beside Charlotte in bed, I told her that I'd had lunch with a woman named Imelda, whom I had met online.

"I hope she's nice," Charlotte said. "I want you to find someone to be with after I'm gone."

* * *

We ordered pizza in for our next date at my studio. Imelda's hair was braided like a long snake; she wore a green miniskirt and red high heels. She told me that after she'd bought the textbooks, the city funding for her medical billing class had unfortunately fallen through. There was no class.

"You don't know the *struggles* that people like me go through—it's humiliating," she said. We'd only just finished our pizza when, as though her presence were a burden on me, she said, "I'll just use your bathroom, and go."

What? Looking sexy as hell, and leaving? Was she depressed over the class cancelation, or just being mean to me?

After coming out of the bathroom, she stood in front of me on the couch, and she pirouetted like a ballerina, revealing that her ass was naked. "I folded my skirt over in front, so you wouldn't guess! I'm a Latin firecracker, baby! Can you can handle it?" She peeked back over her shoulder, and with her hands she spread and un-spread her ass cheeks. "Honey, take it out and I'll masturbate you."

I couldn't resist. I let the sexiest woman I'd ever met use her tiny hands on me.

Over the next couple of months, Imelda came to me at least once a week, but she never allowed complete sex. Instead she fascinated me with never-ending surprises, including sexual ones, like dancing naked above me on the back of the couch, buying sex toys, and sending photos of herself in elaborate outfits.

She told me about her life, and her future plans. Some of what she said made me wonder if it all could be true. When she was ten, a cousin had sneaked into her bedroom and made her masturbate him—until her father found out and beat her cousin with a baseball bat. Her alcoholic father died falling down a flight of stairs. Her husband had tried to "gaslight" her by hiding her favorite things in their attic, to convince her that she was losing her mind, so he could divorce her to be with another woman. "I hired my own psychiatrist to testify in court that I was sane," Imelda proudly told me. "I lay down in the street in front of that other woman's apartment and screamed."

Imelda imagined herself an entrepreneur, constantly concocting big plans for success. With a girlfriend's funding, she would open a shop to sell wedding and party favors that she could make herself. To prove this to me, she gave me one: a wedding favor cleverly fashioned out of a Styrofoam cup, ribbon, lace, and a tiny plastic wedding couple. But the next week, Imelda sadly said that her girlfriend's promise of funding hadn't worked out.

Imelda fascinated me, but I soon realized that I would be a fool to see her as a possible future partner.

She had the naiveté of a child mixed with the cunning of a con artist. When things went wrong, her little-girlish, waiflike look could be heartrending, her diminutive size just adding to the effect. But she had claws. She was litigious, trying to sue for injuries she claimed happened at places she'd worked. And yet she was good-hearted, even generous. She cleaned the apartments of poor elderly neighbors she knew, for free, and made lasagna for them. She arrived for one of our dates carrying a gigantic lasagna.

Then something happened that spurred me to help her. She landed a low-rent, city-subsidized apartment. She might have a fresh start. But the furniture from her marriage was stored, and owing on the payments, she would lose it all. So I decided that I, a hero, would pay off that bill, and generally get her out of debt. I would guarantee Imelda a fresh start. I asked to see all her financial records, and we spread out the papers across my couch. It turned out that she owed on three credit cards. I asked for her promise that there was nothing else. I wrote her a check to pay off all her debts, plus three months' rent and utilities at her new apartment.

Looking back, I'm still not sure what made me do it. I wanted to help someone less fortunate than I. But some of that came from my guilt over my own privileged background. I could afford to help Imelda because my father had left me about a hundred thousand dollars, which I hardly touched. But another thought occurs. Maybe I wanted to feel some power, because I was so powerless to affect what time was doing to Charlotte.

When I gave Imelda the check, I said that we were friends, but *not* a couple. She closed her mouth when I said that, perhaps not believing me. But she took my check.

* * *

It was May, and Charlotte and I were ready to move to Kent. After the confines of the apartment, the country promised fresh air, beauty, and Charlotte's favorite spot, the garden.

Though I had asked Imelda not to call me at Charlotte's, she did just that late one night. On her cell phone, she sounded disoriented, in some kind of daze, as she told me she was on the Brooklyn Bridge. "I'm looking down at the beautiful, inviting water below." She seemed to be flirting with suicide, or was she only playacting? I talked her off the bridge.

Another late night, she called in a different mood. "Honey, I'm butt naked. You do so much for your Charlotte, you need some relaxation. *So take it out, baby.*" I said no, that was over.

I met her once more at my studio, and this time she arrived in dirty jeans and sweatshirt, carrying a bottle of Manischewitz wine in her handbag. Drunkenly she said she owed on a Sears card that she had forgotten about. Years earlier she had invested in materials from Sears to create products. Now a creditor man was knocking on her door, and she was terrified of being thrown into prison.

"They don't do that anymore," I said. I refused to pay her Sears debt. And I refused any sex.

"You promised to marry me," she said.

Had I? Could I have done that one afternoon, drinking too much with her? No. If I had ever given her that impression, I shouldn't have.

On June 1 Charlotte and I left for the country. I was relieved to escape from Manhattan.

30

Saving Graces

In Kent, by this time, Charlotte had accepted her physical limitations, so the bars were not needed around her bed. At night she was able to use a commode that I put only two feet away.

Each morning, Charlotte maintained her daily discipline: she donned her favorite thick robe, got into her wheelchair, and at her desk brushed her teeth over a crescent-shaped plastic trough. She ate oatmeal and a half grapefruit with sugar, and she drank coffee. I often read to her from the *New York Times*, and three days a week Keith came and, weather permitting, they read and talked on the screened porch.

Though I wondered how Imelda was doing, I considered the book on that crazy adventure closed. I was more grateful than ever for my solid, loving, and sane life with Charlotte.

She was even more beautiful to me now. The summer before, we had hired Debby, a hairdresser friend of Wendy's, to cut Charlotte's hair, but now we just let it grow. I loved the wilder, tussled white hair that framed her bright, fragile face.

In her wheelchair Charlotte would make what she called "an appearance" at our monthly writing meetings, to say hello to her friends. Her old friend Joe Tasman came for occasional visits. As well as the reading sessions, TV provided some entertainment.

But Charlotte refused to visit her favorite place, the garden, because she was afraid that ticks might give her Lyme disease again. So, with

Keith, I devised a plan. We assured Charlotte that, up in her wheelchair, her shoes sprayed with DEET, she would be safe. And I opened the front door, and Keith rolled her out and down the little hill, past the silo to the garden.

"Ah, the garden," she said with a grateful sigh.

As though on cue, a great spangled fritillary fluttered above the flowers. We pointed it out. "My favorite, yes," said Charlotte, even though she probably couldn't see it.

We needed a snack to complete this picture, so I asked Charlotte what she wanted.

"Blue Stilton cheese on toast! Put chives from the garden on it." On our drive out of the city, we had stopped at a specialty store, Melange, and bought the Blue Stilton. So I picked the tender green shoots of chives, ran up to the house, and rushed back with food and ice water.

"Mmm, good. We've invented a sandwich," said Charlotte. "Don't forget to write down the recipe."

A few minutes later, though, I noticed how pale and tired Charlotte looked, her eyes dazed and cloudy. She was exhausted for our sakes, convincing us that she was enjoying herself. Time to leave.

* * *

Sometime in July, Charlotte surprised me by saying, as we lay in bed, "Maybe we should get married, after all."

"Maybe we should," I said.

Maybe we could get a justice of the peace to come to us. But doing it now would require a major effort. Charlotte spoke of marriage out of love, I knew; but how much might it also be to leave me more money, as her husband? I would get plenty, anyway. We were already "married" in the most important sense.

On another evening, I told Charlotte, "I love you more than anyone, ever."

"I love you more than anyone, ever," she said.

* * *

A few days later, Charlotte told me, "I want to smell the fir tree this Christmas, before I give up." She had sometimes said that she hoped to die in her sleep, an easier way to go. Now she admitted to me, "I'm scared."

"I'm scared, too," I said.

Holding my hand, she said, "The worst thing is that when I'm gone, I won't know what happens to you."

Fortunately, each night we had a kind of ritual before sleep that settled us down. We let our imaginations create our nightly recitation.

Charlotte had seen, when she was young, Houdini perform his escape from the water box on stage. She revered him for his courage, and also for his skepticism about spiritualist charlatans. But she respected his promise to try to contact his wife after he died, enhanced by his having a phone interred with his body after death. Charlotte did not believe in an afterlife, but she liked the hope. So each night we started our recitation with Houdini.

"We won't forget Houdini, who won't forget us," I began.

"Houdini," repeated Charlotte.

"Our butterflies," I said, and together we recited our butterfly trilogy:

"Great spangled fritillary . . .

Tiger-striped swallowtail . . .

Mourning cloak. . . ."

Then, together, we imagined Charlotte's solo trip on the side-wheeler when she was twelve, except in our fantasy, I was there too, beside her. "We're on the side-wheeler. Blue sky with a few white clouds, and dolphins are swimming in the water." It was our imagined afterlife, and in it we were timeless, and the same age.

"Side-wheeler," repeated Charlotte.

* * *

As July came around, each week Louise arrived to weed the garden, with me as her assistant.

Gardening was Louise's passion. Plants appealed to her belief in the life force, even while she was a tough realist. She admired Charlotte, having once told me, "Charlotte walked up that steep hill with me, and she talked all the time, never got out of breath. Lots of much younger people couldn't do that." Another Louise observation had been, "Charlotte is a person who can dish it out, *and* she can take it. There are very few people like that."

I hated weeding. Louise waded in, squatted, and got to work. I mimicked her but wasn't as efficient. As our pile of pulled weeds grew, I'd load them into the iron-mesh basket and drag it to the far fence and toss the weeds over. Then back to do more. Louise was giving me lessons in hard, patient, steady physical work. My parents' world of work had been mostly about the "higher" calling of doing fine art, and even that was more about inspiration than sweat. But by living with Charlotte into her ancient age, I was learning about the art of living, by working hard to try and help her.

At last Louise stood up, "I guess we can leave the vines for the next time."

* * *

In early August a small package arrived in the mail. It was from Imelda—either I'd given her the Kent address, or she'd found us out. Charlotte's name was above mine on the package, which turned out to contain a box of Werther's old-fashioned hard candies. The note said, "Charlotte, I hope you like these candies. Imelda." Because the gift seemed well intentioned, I felt I should give it to Charlotte.

She loved the candy. Imelda's generous side was successful.

Shortly after that, in Charlotte's room, the phone rang and I picked up. "Can I please say hello to Charlotte?" asked Imelda. Since she was beside me, and liked the candy, I handed Charlotte the phone. I was close enough to hear both voices.

"Thank you so much, the candy is very good," said Charlotte.

"I'm glad, Charlotte. How is the country?"

"A farmhouse, very nice. How are you?"

"Charlotte—can I tell you something?"

"Yes."

"Peter forgot that I love him."

"He what?"

"He forgot that I love him."

Angrily Charlotte shouted into the phone, "He would *never* do that!" and she handed the phone back to me.

"Time to say goodbye, Imelda," I said.

"I'll call you later."

"Please, don't."

I hung up, and said, "She's nuts."

"She loves you," said Charlotte.

We never talked about Imelda again. I had already admitted to Charlotte how much money, tens of thousands of dollars, I had given to her. "Too much," was her comment, but she was not upset, and did not say I was a fool. Charlotte, I suspect, did not want to waste her remaining energy worrying about such things—it took all she had to keep on approaching the age of one hundred.

Imelda had been like an addiction—as a sexy woman, but also as a puzzle that I couldn't resist trying to figure out. I would never know for sure how much she had loved me or tried to con me. But I had been prideful to think that I could elicit or expect reason from someone who was likely mentally ill.

Imelda called again while I was making dinner.

"Peter, I'm at Petaluma. Our favorite restaurant—you hear the people in the background? Peter, how are you? I met a man at the bar who wants to take me to a hotel. Do you think I should?"

"That's up to you. What do you mean?"

"I'm going to turn a trick, Peter, because you won't help me. A girl has to make a living somehow."

Was she bluffing? I thought so, but didn't know.

"I hope you don't do that," I said.

"What's a poor girl to do, Peter? I have to go now. Bye."

31

Sunset of Butterflies

It was the second week of August, and clouds had been building all afternoon. I sat alone out on the porch in the dusk as rain started to fall. I'd neglected to clean out the gutters for too long. In a matter of moments, soft rain became hard rain, a chorus of sound, and in the porch light's glow, I saw sheets of water separated by the wind. The wind wafted cool air and wetness through the screens to my face, so refreshing—nature taking me out of the present to a strong memory.

I'd been six years old when the hurricane of 1955 hit New England, killing numbers of people. Out wading in a small stream, I was nearly swept off my feet. A family friend's house by a river was washed away, and we took in his family. My dog Rex, the family dog, wandered away in the storm and never returned.

Thunder and lightning returned me to the porch, and my present age, fifty-three. I thought of Charlotte, safe in her room. In her, I had found a fellow traveler in time and space. Other people voyaged out across the physical world in search of their identity, but I had circled more inwardly, and back to my own parents' house. But I had brought with me my dearest person.

A violent bolt of lightning made me jump—I should go check on Charlotte. It was dinnertime. I made a baked potato for her, soft and soaked with high-calorie butter, as she liked it. Charlotte's eyesight and shaky hands made it difficult for her to eat, so I spoon-fed her.

"Mmm, it tastes good," she said.

I admired how she took such pleasure in her simple meal. I thought of the movie *Driving Miss Daisy*, when the two old friends—the elderly woman and her former chauffeur— are together at her rest home. Hoke, her best friend, feeds Miss Daisy forkfuls of good pie, and, without pretense, she loves being fed.

* * *

The next morning I looked in on Charlotte to find her wide-eyed in bed, her right arm stretched out at an odd angle. Desperately she said, "I have to go to the bathroom, but I can't get up."

I lifted Charlotte—her right arm around my neck, her left arm and leg limp—and lowered her onto her commode.

She'd had a stroke.

I thought at first that I should call an ambulance. But an EMT crew would likely carry her into the cramped, frightening space of the ambulance to rush her to the hospital. After a moment, I lifted her back into bed. She looked relieved simply to have peed, but what should I do? My gut feeling was that the stroke was over, the damage already done. What would be the point of a torturous ride, and the hospital? My mind raced until I made the decision: at four months from one hundred, stay at home.

Others might second-guess me. Later, someone told me that an ambulance crew might have administered a drug that reduced stroke damage; but that window of opportunity was short. Charlotte must have felt stunned that she could not move her left arm and leg, but she could think and talk, and she was not in pain. Stay at home.

Charlotte and I had been together long enough to not live by others' lights. I called for a visiting nurse, who arrived within the hour.

The nurse confirmed the stroke and arranged for a home health-care worker to start that day. Charlotte was fully aware that she'd had a stroke, and she quietly let herself be cared for.

I called several local doctors to arrange a house visit, but none would come. One way or the other, I would find one. Meanwhile, I began my new education. I thought that diapers made sense, but the nurse said to keep a dry pad under her, and use a bedpan. A little movement could stave off bedsores. Baby food in jars, for now, was best, and fortunately Charlotte liked the peach, apple, and banana. I learned to lift her forward with my arm under her back, so drinking ice water wouldn't choke her. I needed to learn a lot, because, as with the hip and the Lyme, Charlotte wanted only me with her at night.

Exasperated by searching for a local doctor, I called Dr. Wendy in New York. Ridiculously, I offered to pay her expenses to come to Connecticut. Of course she couldn't do that; she said I should transport Charlotte to Manhattan. There, Dr. Wendy would gladly monitor Charlotte personally at home. Who was I to argue with that?

I arranged the ambulance ride, but so Charlotte wouldn't worry, I kept it to myself until Charlotte could hear the plan from Dr. Wendy herself. I called the doctor's office, but she happened to be at the hospital seeing patients there.

"Sorry, Charlotte, at the moment, Dr. Wendy is at the hospital, but she thinks we should go to the city."

I hadn't thought she could, but Charlotte sat up and loudly said, "I don't want to go to New York!"

I appealed to her. Surely Dr. Wendy knew best.

"No! *She's* at the hospital, so *she's* the one who's sick, not me!"

Was Charlotte confused from her stroke? More likely, she knew her own mind. Charlotte was happier in the Kent house— this was her home, too.

I found a doctor in the neighboring town of Sharon, a specialist in older people, who came to us. He suggested the stroke happened when a blood clot traveled from her irregularly beating heart to her brain. I peppered him with so many questions that he stared hard at me and asked, "What's this? Are you trying to become a nurse in a week?"

I wilted, afraid that he was criticizing me.

"That's a lot of work," he said. "You're a good man. You must love her very much."

He suggested that Charlotte could recover, if things went well. Mild physical therapy might begin soon. This was the first good news I'd heard lately.

But for now, it was all about the new routine: baby food, ice water, a fresh pad and the bed pan, tending to one bedsore, reading to her. She slept a lot. Talkative Charlotte was no longer a talker.

One late night, Charlotte began moaning in the most disturbing way. She seemed caught between being awake and asleep, and I worried that she was in pain. She asked me to stay close at night, so I bedded down on the couch near her bed. I called my own doctor to ask him about her moaning. Brad said it was called "sundowning," not painful, and in itself, not a problem. I dreamt that I was traveling alone on a train before it stopped, and I got out and saw a red and orange sunset— the sun going down. Sundowning?

Then Charlotte's moaning stopped. She seemed more comfortable.

There was a mystery of time going on. First thing in the morning, several times, Charlotte looked wide-eyed up at me and said, "I had a stroke," as though it had just happened that night. Had she lost track of time? Maybe this was a godsend, to help her endure what otherwise might feel like an excruciatingly long time immobilized in bed? Our several weeks so far, for me, had felt like a year. Another odd thing was how Charlotte would look at me with big, curious eyes and recite the letters, "A . . . B . . . C." Only those letters. Were those letters code, was she trying to tell me something? Or was she simply testing her memory of the alphabet? I didn't know.

Charlotte's new doctor sent a physical therapist, who showed me how to gently move Charlotte's bad arm and leg. We actually got Charlotte to sit up on the edge of her bed. I felt a rush of relief: Charlotte would recover!

Every night I would read aloud Beatrix Potter's *Peter Rabbit*, just as Charlotte's mother had read it to her as a little girl at the beginning of the twentieth century. It calmed both of us. After reading, I would lie down next to Charlotte, like always—but I had to brace my forearm on the bedside table so as not to fall out of bed, since she couldn't move over for me. We recited our "butterflies," only now I said most of the words.

"Great spangled fritillary . . . tiger-striped swallowtail . . . mourning cloak."

"Mourning cloak," Charlotte might repeat.

"Side-wheeler . . . dolphins in the water."

"Houdini."

"Houdini."

* * *

Then, suddenly, Charlotte's heels turned dark. She had to wear horrible big blue "shoes" so her feet wouldn't touch the sheets. The visiting nurse warned me that it was a sign of the end.

I took a time-out to go to the garden, with a pad of watercolor paper. While sitting in front of the flowers, a story came to me that I wrote on the pad, leaving spaces for illustrations. It was like a children's book story. A young sea snail is caught in a hurricane that blows his shell off, so he is left naked and defenseless against many enemies—a lobster, a stingray, a seagull. Somehow he survives until he finally meets a friendly hermit crab, who gives the snail his own shell for shelter.

It dawned on me that I was writing about losing Charlotte. But what shell would I find?

After midnight on September 23, 2002, Charlotte was still awake, but seemed apart, in her own world. Her good hand, the right hand, was curling in on itself. I managed to lie down beside her, and say our prayers, but I didn't know if she heard me.

So I sat in a chair by her bed. I drank some gin, and smoked a few of her leftover Camels. I kept checking to see that she was breathing. Around three or four o'clock, I got my watercolor pad and began illustrating the story I'd written in the garden. After each sketch, I leaned close to Charlotte's face. Her breath was shallow. I kept drawing.

After I drew an octopus chasing the sea snail on page seven, I leaned close: Charlotte had stopped breathing. Her chest wasn't moving. I put her Venetian lipstick holder's mirror to her lips: it didn't cloud.

I'd entered a world of impossibility and had the sensation that no air was filling my own chest. I paced around Charlotte's room.

Whatever "art" does for us, I felt an impulse to fetch my camera to take pictures of Charlotte. Her eyes closed, she looked angelic with her white hair across the pillow. Now I could take a deeper breath.

For an instant, I imagined I would get her breakfast so she could eat at her desk.

It was getting light outside.

I went to the garden. Charlotte had often said, *Time must have a stop.* I would need an infinite amount of time to understand this finite fact. But I had only an hour or two before the day would take over, forcing me back into normal life. Time would speed on, but how would I bring Charlotte with me?

The best I could do was to pick some flowers from the garden—marigolds, butterfly bush flowers, asters, and goldenrod— and bring them to her.

I placed the bouquet on Charlotte's chest.

The day was here.

Afterword

There was champagne and caviar at the service for Charlotte at the house, which sixty people of all ages attended.

For a year, I kept saying goodbye to her in my dreams. After a meal with Charlotte, I fell into a crevice of rushing water that drowned me. In another dream, Charlotte said goodbye before she walked away into a dark landscape. Later, she appeared as a pond creature who descended underwater to hibernate. In another dream, I drove my car under a stormy sky when she appeared by the road and told me, "Everything will be all right."

One morning I found a hummingbird trapped inside the screens of the porch. To my amazement, I was able to hold the tiny bird's green, pulsing body in my bare hand, to carry it to the door. I opened my hand—it rocketed out into the world. I felt as though I'd freed Charlotte.

I wish I had learned even more from Charlotte, but I tell myself I learned enough to continue on my own. Two years after the service, to work on this book, I entered the Bennington Writing Seminars, an MFA program. There I met a woman of my own age, and we are now a couple.

Sketches of Charlotte

In a way words can't, a selection of my drawings shows Charlotte in all her vitality. I loved sketching her, often on a paper placemat in a good restaurant as we enjoyed martinis and raw oysters— those were the best of times.

In order:

Serious Charlotte • On the phone • In Woodstock • Dinner at L'Absinthe • Martini and a Camel • Loving chocolate • Lyme disease • Classic Charlotte.